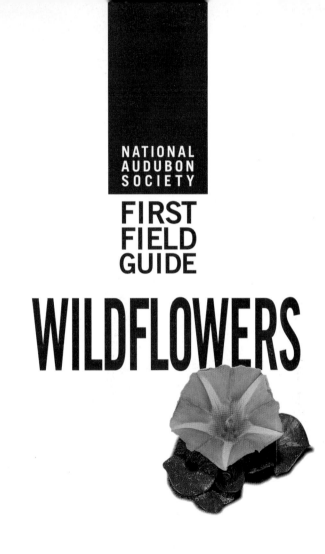

NATIONAL
AUDUBON
SOCIETY

FIRST
FIELD
GUIDE

WILDFLOWERS

NATIONAL AUDUBON SOCIETY

FIRST FIELD GUIDE

WILDFLOWERS

Written by
Susan Hood

Scholastic Inc.
New York   Toronto   London   Auckland   Sydney

The National Audubon Society, established in 1905, has 550,000 members and more than 500 chapters nationwide. Its mission is to conserve and restore natural ecosystems, focusing on birds and other wildlife, and these guides are part of that mission. Celebrating the beauty and wonders of nature, Audubon looks toward its second century of educating people of all ages. For information about Audubon membership, contact:

National Audubon Society

700 Broadway

New York, NY 10003-9562

212-979-3000   800-274-4201

http://www.audubon.org

LIBRARY OF CONGRESS CATALOGING-IN-PUBLICATION DATA
Hood, Susan.
National Audubon Society first field guide to wildflowers/Susan Hood.
p. cm.
Includes index.
Summary: Provides an overview of wildflowers and where they grow, with
specific information about individual species.
ISBN 0-590-05486-4   ISBN 0-590-05464-3
1. Wild flowers—North America—Identification—Juvenile literature.
2. Wild flowers—Identification—Juvenile literature.
[1. Wild flowers.] I. National Audubon Society.
II. Title.
QK110.H66   1998
582.13' 097—dc21   97-17992 CIP AC

ISBN 0-590-05464-3 (HC)
ISBN 0-590-05486-4 (PB)

10 9 8 7 6 5 4 3 2 1   8 9/9 0/0 01 02

Printed in Hong Kong
First printing, April 1998

Contents

About this book

Whether you are looking at wildflowers in your own backyard, taking a walk in the woods, or hiking in the mountains, this book will help you look at wildflowers the way a naturalist does. The book has four parts:

Orange Hawkweed page 96

PART 1: The world of wildflowers tells you about the many different kinds of wildflowers, examines their anatomy, describes how seeds and fruits are formed, explores the ingenious methods plants use to spread their seeds, and explains how wildflowers are named by botanists.

PART 2: How to look at wildflowers gives you the information you need to begin identifying wildflowers. You learn fascinating facts about their colors, shapes, and scents; find out when they bloom and where they live; and learn about the plights of several endangered North American wildflowers.

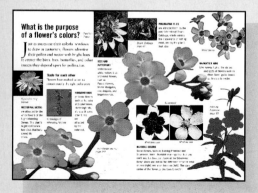

PART 3: The field guide

includes detailed descriptions and dramatic photographs of 50 common North American wildflowers. In addition, this section provides helpful shorter descriptions accompanied by photographs of over 125 other important species.

How to use the reference section

The Glossary beginning on the opposite page contains terms used by botanists and naturalists. If you run across a word in this book that you don't understand, check the glossary for a definition. Also in this section is a listing of Resources, including books, web sites, and organizations devoted to North American wildflowers. Finally, there is an Index of all the species covered in the Field Guide section of this book.

The 50 state flowers

Every state has its official flower. All 50 state flowers appear on the next five pages listed in alphabetical order by state. If you live in Missouri, for example, go across the list to the states beginning with the letter M, the state flower for Missouri is the Red Hawthorn. Like the Red Hawthorn, many other state flowers are flowering trees and not wildflowers. (Wildflowers are defined in this book as flowering plants—including shrubs, vines, and cacti—but not trees and garden flowers.) The names on this list are those used by the states and may not be the common names used by botanists.

PART 4: The reference section

at the back of the book includes a helpful glossary of technical terms used by botanists; an illustrated directory of the 50 state flowers; lists of useful books, Web sites, and organizations; and an index of species covered in the field guide.

The spotter's guide is

a handy, pocket-sized card picturing 50 commonly seen wildflowers of North America. Take it with you whenever you go for a walk.

7

How to be a naturalist

Anaturalist studies nature to understand how it works. You don't need a fancy diploma or a laboratory lined with scientific equipment to be a naturalist—you need only your senses, your curiosity, and the ability to spot clues and ask questions.

Take a closer look.

A good observer uses his or her ears, nose, hands, and mind. How good an observer are you? Look at a wildflower. Then close your eyes. How many petals did it have? What color was it? What did it smell like? What shape were its leaves? Were they smooth and waxy or covered with tiny hairs? Did you see seeds? These are some of the clues a naturalist uses to identify a flower.

YOU CAN CONTRIBUTE.

More than half a million plants have been discovered to date, but scientists expect to find at least half a million more. Who knows—you might be the one to make the next great discovery!

Alice Eastwood (1859–1953) was a self-taught botanist who traveled thousands of miles collecting 340,000 plants for study. She rescued more than 1,200 plants from the San Francisco earthquake and fire of 1906. A lily, fuchsia, and orchid are all named after her.

Shooting Stars

The most important things to take with you when you look for wildflowers are this field guide and a camera (or a notebook and pencils) to record what you see.

Rules for a naturalist

- Never taste a plant. Some are deadly poisonous.
- Look carefully at a plant before you touch it. Some have stinging prickles or poisonous barbs.
- When you pick a flower you destroy its ability to produce seeds. It's better to take a photograph instead.
- It's usually against the law to take anything from a national or state park. If you're unsure, check with a ranger.
- If you're going on a nature walk, check with your parents and take a buddy along. It can be dangerous to hike alone.
- Never litter. Leave the wilderness just as you found it.

How many kinds of wildflowers are there?

At least half of the 500,000 plant species known produce flowers. There are more than 22,000 species of wildflowers in the United States alone (not including gardeners' flowers, trees, and shrubs).

Great Lobelia

Beyond the rainbow

Wildflowers come in nearly any color you can name.

Making scents

The sweet scent of purple violets is used to make expensive perfume, but only flies would want a whiff of the purplish-brown Skunk Cabbage, which smells like its namesake.

Skunk Cabbage page 47

Wolffia

Record-breakers

The world's largest flower is the reddish-orange Rafflesia, found in the jungles of Southeast Asia. It can grow as large as three feet across—the size of a truck tire! North America's green Wolffia flower is the smallest flower; it's no bigger than the head of a pin.

Rafflesia

Silversword

More than a pretty face

Part of the charm of wildflowers comes from the history surrounding them. They've been used as medicines, folk remedies, and more.

Fleabane was used to repel fleas in the days before insecticides.

Daisy Fleabane

Growing high and low

Reddish-purple Silversword thrives only in the ashes atop old Hawaiian volcanoes. Green Eelgrass blooms in the salty seas of our northern coasts.

Bloodroot has underground stems, called rhizomes, containing a blood-red juice used by Native Americans as a dye for clothing.

Bloodroot page 51

Foxglove leaves are poisonous and yet provide an important medicine called digitalis, used for people with heart disorders.

Foxglove

Milkweed pods were collected by children during World War II. The floss, five times as buoyant as cork, was used to stuff life jackets.

Milkweed pods page 99

What is a wildflower?

Skunk Cabbage page 47

Wildflowers aren't just rare, fragrant beauties on the forest floor. They're also stinky Skunk Cabbages, meat-eating Venus Flytraps, and towering sunflowers. Some say a wildflower is a wild flowering plant without woody stem or trunk. In this book, wildflowers are flowering plants (including shrubs, vines, and cacti), but not trees and gardeners' flowers.

Black-eyed Susan page 77

All-American natives vs. immigrants

Wild rose

Cacti, Black-eyed Susans, and Bloodroots are native plants that first grew in North America. Other flowers, such as forget-me-nots, are imports from other parts of the world.

Anatomy of a wildflower

Despite their obvious differences in appearance, most wildflowers have the same set of "body parts."

FLOWERS produce seeds.

STEMS carry water and nutrients from the roots up to the leaves.

LEAVES take in sunlight to make the plant's food in a process called photosynthesis.

ROOTS anchor the plant in the soil and draw water and nutrients from the soil into the plant.

Cultivated rose

Taming wildflowers

Once all plants were wild. Over the years, people have developed new plants with showier blooms or better resistance to disease. These are called cultivated plants. Elegant garden tea roses are simply cultivated cousins of wild roses.

13

The parts of a flower

Most flowers have male and female parts. The male part is called the stamen, and the female part is known as the pistil.

ANTHER

STIGMA

Pistil

Usually in the center of the flower, the pistil has three main parts. At the top is a sticky opening, the stigma. This leads to a tube called the style. At the bottom is a tiny chamber, an ovary. Inside the ovary are ovules, the plant's eggs.

Stamen

The number of stamens may vary from species to species, but each stamen has two parts: a stalk called a filament and a tip called an anther. The anther produces pollen.

FILAMENT

Wood Lily blossom page 75   disk flowers

Flower variations

Many flowers, such as the Wood
Lily, have pistils surrounded by rings
of petals, stamens, and sepals, but
there are countless variations on this
theme. Composite flowers, such as
Purple Coneflowers, have floral
heads composed of hundreds of disk
flowers; these are surrounded by
sterile ray flowers that have petals
but no pistils or stamens.

ray flower

*Bee pollinating
Purple
Coneflower*

Petal

Petals are usually the most colorful
parts of the flower. They are the
flower's billboard, advertising tasty
nectar or pollen.
Petals also serve as
landing platforms
for pollinators.

Cultivated rose

Sepals

Cattails

Sepals

Sepals are
usually green and
are found under-
neath the flower.
The sepals together are
known as the calyx. The
first part to form on a bud,
the calyx protects the
growing flower. In some
plants such as the Lily, the spread
the petals and sepals look alike.

MALE AND FEMALE FLOWERS

Some flowers, like cattails, have female parts
on one flower and male parts on another.

A seed is born

Every flower has a life-or-death mission: to make new seeds. Without seeds most species would not survive. There are two steps in making seeds: pollination and fertilization.

Pollinating Sphinx Moth

Pollinating Spicebush Swallowtail

Bunchberry fruits

Pollination

When wind, water, birds, or insects move pollen from one flower to the stigma of another, the process is called cross-pollination. When pollen from a plant falls on the stigma of the same plant, it's called self-pollination.

Fertilization

Fertilization takes place once pollination occurs. Pollen landing on a stigma produces a tiny tube that grows down the style. Male cells pass through the tube and combine with ovules in the ovary. The process of fertilization can take a few hours or a few months.

HOW SEEDS AND FRUITS DEVELOP

Once fertilization takes place, the flower withers and dies. One or more seeds grow in the ovary, depending on the number of eggs or ovules, and the ovary develops into a fruit or fruits (such as the bright red ones of Bunchberry), or a seed pod (such as the slender ones of Fireweed) that shelter seeds until they are full grown.

16

What's in a seed?

A seed is like a mobile home. Inside is the passenger—a tiny plant called an embryo—and a supply of food packed by the parent flower. A seed has everything the young plant needs to put down roots and start a new life in a different location.

Aster seed

Great Ragweed seed

Verbena seed

Black-eyed Susan seed

Buttercup seed

MAKING SEEDS TWO DIFFERENT WAYS

The Common Blue Violet spreads very quickly to fill any available spaces. It produces seeds by cross-pollination as bees carry pollen from one of its delicate white or lavender flowers to another. It also generates seeds by self-pollination with tiny flowers under its leaves that never open to insects. The process of cross-pollination with showy flowers happens early in the year. Self-pollination with the smaller flowers takes place later, ensuring that one way or another these hardy wildflowers will continue to flourish.

Staying alive

Some seeds stay alive only a few days after they mature. Other seeds need a rest, or dormant period, before they sprout. The record for the longest-lasting seed is held by Arctic Lupine seeds that sprouted after being frozen underground for 10,000 years.

Arctic Lupine

Common Blue Violet
page 49

What is a fruit?

Fruit

Seed

Cherry cross section

Cherry

Say the word "fruit" and you may think of good things to eat like peaches or cherries. A botanist thinks of fruit as the part of the flower in which seeds grow—the ovary. Cherries are fruits, but so are papery milkweed pods.

Fleshy fruits

Most of us are familiar with fleshy tree fruits such as peaches, plums, and cherries. The fleshy fruits of wildflowers often are berries, such as the poisonous ones of Jack-in-the-Pulpits.

Jack-in-the-Pulpit berries

Jack-in-the-Pulpit page 46

A BERRY OF MANY FRUITS

Each segment on a raspberry is a fruit that develops from the many ovaries in a single flower.

Color changes

Fleshy fruits change color as the seed inside matures. The bright color, soft flesh, and sweet taste tell animals, "Come and get me!" Until then, fruits stay green, hard, and sour, camouflaging immature seeds against green leaves and discouraging nibbling.

PEAS ARE SEEDS.
Peas grow in green, moist fruits called pods.

Pea pod

DRY FRUITS

When ripe, milkweed pods split, releasing hundreds of brown seeds, each with a tuft of about 900 silky hairs that catch the breeze.

Milkweed pods page 99

When is a seed not a seed?

Sunflower seeds aren't seeds at all. They are hard dry fruits called achenes. Each has a single seed inside. The achene doesn't split to release the seed; the seed breaks the fruit's walls as it grows.

HIP, HIP

On a wild rose, the stem's top enlarges, forming a cup around the cluster of pistils. This cup ripens to become a bright red rose hip holding several hard, dry fruits, or achenes.

Rose hip page 130

HAVE PARACHUTE, WILL TRAVEL.

A dandelion achene's parachute is called a pappus. Each achene has tiny hooks that help anchor it to the ground when it lands.

Pappus

Achene

Common Buttercup page 72

HEART OF A BUTTERCUP

The pistils of a buttercup develop into a cluster of hard dry fruits or achenes. When ripe, the cluster breaks apart into individual achenes that look like seeds.

19

Jewelweed

How do seeds spread?

A year ago some thistles were growing in the empty lot next door. This spring they're in your garden. How did they get there? Flowers can't move; they're anchored in place by their roots. Flower seeds, however, can travel with the help of animals, wind, and water.

BEWARE EXPLOSIVES!

Jewelweed, also known as Touch-me-not, has a seed pod with straps that stretch like rubber bands as it grows. Once seeds ripen, the pod explodes at the slightest touch, tossing seeds six feet or more.

Tumbleweed

GONE WITH THE WIND

Breezes can waft seeds across your yard; a gale can carry them many miles. Tumbleweeds snap off at their roots after flowering and cartwheel across the western landscape at speeds of up to 70 miles per hour—spreading seeds as they go.

STOWAWAYS

Many wildflowers now found here immigrated with colonists. Common Plantain was a stowaway mixed in with hay. Native Americans nicknamed it Whiteman's Foot and used it to detect the presence of settlers.

Common Plantain

Butter-and-Eggs

INVITED GUESTS

Colonists prized certain European plants for their culinary and medicinal value. They packed mint and Butter-and-Eggs (thought to cure jaundice and eye infections) to take to America.

DRIFTERS

Milkweed and water lily seeds can wash away in a rainstorm or float miles across the surface of a lake or pond.

SPREAD BY BIRDS

When birds eat fruit, they may swallow seeds that then come out in droppings, often miles from the plant. Charles Darwin once grew 80 plants from mud scraped off a bird's foot.

HITCHHIKERS

Burdock seeds have tiny hooks that latch onto passing animals and people. In 1957 burrs caught on the clothes of a Swiss engineer and became his inspiration for a new invention—Velcro!

Great Burdock

ROOM TO GROW

Seeds must leave home to survive. If all of a plant's seeds fell to the ground directly beneath the parent wildflower, there wouldn't be enough soil, water, or sunlight for them.

Spreading without seeds

Many seed-producing wildflowers can also reproduce by growing roots, runners, and shoots. This process, called vegetative propagation, produces clones and comes in handy when farmers want to duplicate a particularly hardy or attractive plant.

New strawberry plants develop from runners.

21

What's in a name?

CAROLUS LINNAEUS

ots of confusion! Take Queen Anne's Lace, so named for its lacy blossoms. Others call it Bird's Nest because it curls into a nest shape. Still others call it Wild Carrot. Common names vary, so scientists use scientific names to identify living things. Some scientists in different parts of the world may have never heard of Queen Anne's Lace, but all will know the plant by its scientific name, *Daucus carota*.

Queen Anne's Lace
Scientific name: *Daucus carota*
page 66

The scientific naming system was developed in the mid-1700s by a Swedish botanist named Carolus Linnaeus. Still in use today, his system is called binomial nomenclature, which means "two-part naming."

How scientists sort names

Since Linnaeus, scientists have sorted all living things into categories using a system called taxonomy or classification. It's similar to the way librarians sort books in different sections and on different shelves.

Scientific names

All known plants and animals are given a two-part name, usually in Latin or ancient Greek because they were the languages used by scientists in Linnaeus' time. The first part of a scientific name identifies the flower's genus (group). The second part is for the species (kind) and is usually a descriptive word or adjective. No two species have the same pair of words.

Four plants classified

See how a buttercup is classified below. You'll notice that buttercups, larkspurs, and flowering magnolia trees have a lot in common. All three are flowering plants with similar structures. Pine trees are also part of the plant kingdom, but they aren't flowering plants. They bear cones containing naked seeds, which are not enclosed by a protective covering or a fruit.

	Common Buttercup	Spring Larkspur	Southern Magnolia tree	Eastern White Pine
KINGDOM	Plantae	Plantae	Plantae	Plantae
DIVISION	Anthophyta	Anthophyta	Anthophyta	Tracheophyta
CLASS	Dicotyledonae	Dicotyledonae	Dicotyledonae	Gymnospermae
ORDER	Ranales	Ranales	Ranales	Pinales
FAMILY	Ranunculaceae	Ranunculaceae	Magnoliaceae	Pinaceae
GENUS	*Ranunculus*	*Delphinium*	*Magnolia*	*Pinus*
SPECIES	*acris*	*tricorne*	*grandiflora*	*strobus*

What is the purpose of a flower's colors?

Passion-flower

Just as stores use their colorful windows to draw in customers, flowers advertise their pollen and nectar with bright hues to attract the birds, bats, butterflies, and other insects they depend upon for pollination.

Made for each other

Flowers have evolved colors to attract exactly the right pollinators.

Night-blooming Cereus

NOCTURNAL MOTHS

are attracted by the white flowers of the Night-blooming Cereus. The plant's bright red berries lure birds that help spread its seeds.

Hummingbird pollinating fuchsia

HUMMINGBIRDS

pollinate flowers such as fuchsias and columbines. Hummingbirds, along with some other birds, are attracted by the color red.

BEES AND BUTTERFLIES

prefer to visit white, yellow, blue, and violet flowers, such as Passionflowers, Marsh Marigolds, snapdragons, and forget-me-nots.

True Forget-me-not
page 142

POLLINATING FLIES

are attracted both by the purplish color of Skunk Cabbage, which mimics the appearance of rotting meat, and by the plant's foul odor.

Skunk Cabbage
page 47

Wood Sorrel

NAVIGATION AIDS

Like runway lights, the stripes and spots of flowers such as Wood Sorrel guide insect pollinators to nectar.

Silverweed

Evening
Primrose
page 90

What bees see

What we see

INVISIBLE COLORS

Some flowers, such as Evening Primrose and Silverweed, have ultraviolet markings that humans can't see, but bees can. Look at the Silverweed flower above and notice the difference between what we see (right) and what bees see (left). The dark center of the flower guides bees to nectar.

Texas Bluebonnet page 141

Wildflowers come in a variety of shapes

Tubes, bells, spikes, stars, funnels, trumpets, darts, pipes, baggy pants, elephant heads—flowers have these shapes and more. Nature has custom-made each shape to attract desirable pollinators.

Butterfly Weed
page 98

THE MORE, THE MERRIER

Some wildflowers, such as buttercups, have one flower atop one stem. Others, such as Elephant Heads, cluster many tiny flowers together on tall spires, making a greater impression on passing pollinators.

A LONG DRINK

Butterflies and moths have long drinking tubes they unroll to suck up nectar from deep inside tubular flowers.

Common Buttercup page 72

Trumpet Honeysuckle page 104

Common Sunflower page 76

VERSATILE BEES

Undaunted by a wildflower's shape, bees crawl through irises' obstacle courses and rob tubular flowers by making slits in their sides.

TUBES AND TRUMPETS

Trumpet Honeysuckle has long tubular flowers—a fitting match for the long slender beaks and tongues of its pollinator, the hummingbird.

COMPOSITE FLOWERS

Each sunflower head has close to 2,000 flowers— both ray flowers that encircle the head and disk flowers that form the center. With one stop, bees can pollinate lots of flowers!

Elephant Heads page 127

WIDE OPEN SPACES

Flies can't reach nectar inside tubular flowers. They prefer flatter flowers with exposed stamens and pistils, such as butter-cups or Golden Alexanders.

Iris

Golden Alexanders

A close look at wildflower leaves

Jerusalem Artichoke (a toothed leaf) page 77

Wildflower leaves have evolved shapes and arrangements that give them the best exposure to sunlight and reduce wind damage and water loss. The shape and arrangement of leaves vary from species to species, so leaves can help you identify wildflowers, especially before or after they flower.

BEWARE!
Look before you touch. Many leaves, such as the ones on the Stinging Nettle plant, have prickles for self-defense. Some are even poisonous.

Coneflower (a lance-shaped leaf)

Leaf Clues

When examining a leaf, ask yourself:

- Is there one leaf on a stem or many?
- How wide is the leaf?
- Are the edges of the leaf smooth, jagged, or spread out like fingers on a hand?
- What does the leaf feel like? Is it fuzzy, hairy, waxy, or smooth?
- How are the leaves arranged on the stem?

Great Ragweed (a lobed leaf)

28

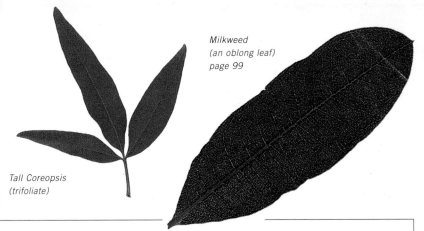

Milkweed
(an oblong leaf)
page 99

Tall Coreopsis
(trifoliate)

FOOD FACTORY

Whatever their shape, most leaves have one thing in common. They make a plant's food (glucose) in a process called photosynthesis, which can be summarized by this formula:

Water + Carbon Dioxide + Sunlight = Glucose (sugar) + Oxygen

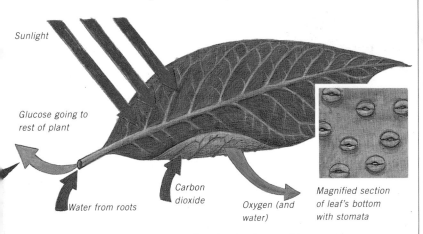

Sunlight

Glucose going to rest of plant

Water from roots

Carbon dioxide

Oxygen (and water)

Magnified section of leaf's bottom with stomata

1. A plant's roots pump water from the soil up into its stems and leaves.
2. A gas in the atmosphere called carbon dioxide enters the leaf through tiny holes (stomata) found on the underside of the leaf.
3. When sunlight shines on tiny green particles (chloroplasts) in a leaf's cells, some of its energy changes water and carbon dioxide in the leaf into oxygen and a sugary food called glucose.
4. The oxygen is given off through the stomata.

29

Purple Trillium page 55

Why do wildflowers have scents?

Bull Thistle page 116

STINKERS

The Purple Trillium has no nectar for bees, but it does offer food for pollen-eating flies. To attract these flies, it emits a stench like dead meat.

A wildflower's scent is often just as important as its color in attracting pollinators best suited for the job. From a range of 30 feet, honeybees notice the flowers with sweet-smelling perfume first. Color and shape become important as the bee flies closer. Different scents attract different pollinators.

SHARP THORNS, SWEET PERFUME

A Bull Thistle's pleasant smell attracts both butterflies and bees.

Red Clover page 120

CLOVER'S LURE

The sweet fragrance of clover attracts bees that use its nectar to produce a fine quality honey.

Jimsonweed page 129

MIDNIGHT AROMA

Night-blooming Jimsonweed has a strong, sweet scent that attracts hawk moths.

Male bee on orchid

TRICKSTERS

Some orchids lure male bees by mimicking the scent of a female bee. The bee lands looking for love and although he finds no female, he picks up pollen, which he then delivers to the next enticing imposter.

ODORLESS BEAUTIES

Flowers, such as fuchsia, which are pollinated by hummingbirds, have little or no scent and lure birds with their bright colors.

California Fuchsia

DEADLY FUMES

The pitcher plant lures insects with a smell of decay. After they tumble in, the plant releases juices that digest its visitors.

WHIFF OF WATER

Ever smell a stagnant pond? That's the scent of the Jack-in-the-Pulpit. It's irresistible to a mosquito.

Jack-in-the-Pulpit page 46

Northern Pitcher Plant page 65

When do wildflowers bloom?

Crimson Columbine

Some wildflowers open in the morning, while others bloom at night. Each year in northern areas, the earliest blossoms appear around Valentine's Day, while late bloomers make a final appearance around Halloween.

Painted Trillium

Name clues

The common names of wildflowers can provide clues to blooming times. Trilliums are called wake robins because they flower in early spring, when robins first appear. Mayapples bloom in May. Flowers aptly called Farewell-to-Spring blossom in June in California and western Canada.

HERE'S THE SUN

The amount of sunlight affects blooming times. Woodland wildflowers such as Bloodroot, trillium, and Wild Columbine burst into bloom from March to May—before forest trees open their leaves and block the sunlight.

VISITING HOURS

Flowers also bloom at times coordinated with the visiting hours of pollinators. Many hummingbird-pollinated flowers bloom during the midsummer northern migration of hummingbirds from the tropics. These flowers close on summer nights, when hummingbirds can't see well enough to fly.

Female Ruby-throated Hummingbird and Bee Balm

32

Water Lily

WATER LILIES
bloom from early in the morning to about noon.

What time is it?

Flowers keep regular hours when it comes to opening their petals. Botanist Carolus Linnaeus proved this by planting a flower clock—a garden with flowers arranged so that you could tell the hour by which flowers were open.

Century Plant

ONCE IN A LIFETIME
Nicknamed century plants, agaves were once thought to take 100 years to flower. In fact, these southwestern desert plants each need between 10 and 50 years to produce a single 30-foot-high flower stalk.

Desert Four O'Clocks

DESERT FOUR O'CLOCKS
bloom just once as the heat of the day subsides until the following morning. Since few desert pollinators are out and about during the intense heat of the day, it makes more sense for these flowers to open their petals at night.

CALIFORNIA POPPIES
unfold their petals at sunrise and close again at night. This protects precious pollen from dew that would spoil it.

California Poppies
page 94

Round-lobed Hepatica

Just as some of us live in the mountains and others prefer homes by the sea, different wildflowers favor different homes or habitats. Some need hot, dry climates; others can't live without soggy soil. There are several major habitats in North America. Each has its own geography and climate with different temperatures, amounts of sunlight, and rainfall. Knowing a wildflower's typical habitat can help you with identification. You won't expect to find a Round-lobed Hepatica in a moist woods or a Venus Flytrap in a desert.

Into the woods

Dutchman's Breeches

In the early spring, forest floors are carpeted with wildflowers. For Bloodroot, Mayapple, Dutchman's Breeches, Wild Blue Phlox, Blue Violets, Hepatica, and Virginia Bluebells, spring is a race against time. They rush to bloom from March to May, before the tree leaves come out and block their sunlight.

The life of a thief

The Mistletoe that people hang at Christmastime lives the life of a thief. It needs no soil, but clings to tree branches and steals its nourishment from them.

Mistletoe

Made in the shade

Striped Coral Root, an orchid, can live in deep, shady woods from May to August because it doesn't need sunlight to make its food. Called a saprophyte because it lacks chlorophyll, this plant takes its nourishment from the partly decayed organic matter called duff on the forest floor.

Striped Coral Root

Prairies and plains

Coneflowers

A century ago our grasslands were home to vast numbers of wildflowers: sunflowers, coneflowers, goldenrod, daisies, and others. Since then, developments, farms, and pesticides have taken their toll.

TALL TO SMALL

In the Midwest, Prairie Coneflowers grow as tall as three feet. As you go farther west, rainfall declines and so does the height of the wildflowers. The Pasqueflower, also known as Prairie Smoke, which grows on the high plains, reaches a height of only ten inches.

Pasqueflower

A WORLD OF GRASS

Grasslands are home to a variety of grasses with names such as Indian Grass, Big Bluestem, and June Grass. Grasses have deep roots to hold moisture and can lie dormant during droughts.

FLOWERS OF THE WIND

Did you know that grasses have flowers? Usually small and inconspicuous, they use the wind for pollination and don't need to be big and showy to attract insects.

Fields, lots, and roadsides

Viper's Bugloss

T hese wayside places are the New World homes of many Old World flowers. Dandelion, Chicory, and Burdock were European natives; they arrived here with the immigrants and then escaped into the wild.

Common St. Johnswort page 88

Chicory

Friends...

Hairy Vetch, found throughout much of North America, is used as fodder for animals and plowed under to add nitrogen to the soil.

Fireweed is often the first plant to take hold after a fire. It stabilizes the soil, then dies back as other plants return.

Chicory dots roadsides and waste places. It has been used to prevent scurvy, and the roots are roasted as a coffee substitute.

...or foes?

Bindweed annoys farmers because it wraps itself around anything nearby, including farm machinery.

Common St. Johnswort, brought from Europe, causes nasty sores in the livestock that eat it.

Viper's Bugloss arrived from Europe as a stowaway in the late 1600s and became a pesky weed on pioneer farms and homesteads.

37

At the water's edge

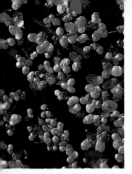

Lesser Duckweed

Y ou might not like getting your feet wet in a swamp or stream, but wetland wildflowers do. Some, such as Pickerelweed, thrive in water, rooted to the muddy bottom. Others, like monkeyflowers, grow along stream banks. Arrowhead and cattails are found at the edges of ponds.

Lewis' Monkeyflower

THE MEAT EATERS

Bogs lack one thing plants need—nitrogen. To make up for missing nitrogen, such plants as the Venus Flytrap, pitcher plants, and sundews are carnivorous; they trap insects as a kind of mineral supplement.

Venus Flytrap
page 64

TWO STRIKES AND...

The Venus Flytrap grows in North and South Carolina. Its leaves are lined with spikes. If an insect touches one, nothing happens; but if it touches another spike within 20 seconds, the lobes snap shut.

DEADLY BAUBLES

Sundew leaves are covered with hairs tipped with shiny beads of "glue" on which insects land and stick fast. Other hairs bend over, entrapping the prey, and digestive juices in the "glue" go to work.

Sea Oats

Round-leaved Sundew page 65

Water Lily

NOT TRUE LILIES

Water Lilies belong to their own flower family, which includes the lotus. They float in shallow ponds and swamps, buoyed by air sacs in their petals and sepals.

By the sea

Wild roses, Silverweed, and Sea Oats are among the few plants that can cope with the salt water, bright sunshine, and wild winds of the seashore. They perform a valuable service in anchoring the otherwise shifting sand dunes. Cordgrass grows in salt marshes because its leaves can expel salt.

Pickerelweed page 138

Living in the desert

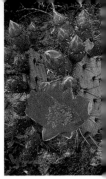

Could you survive months without water, standing in the blazing sun all day and shivering in chilly temperatures all night? Desert plants can. They have ways of coping with long droughts and wildly varying temperatures.

*Prickly Pear
page 70*

TITANS OF THE DESERT

A Saguaro cactus can produce 40 to 50 million seeds in its lifetime, grow as tall as a five-story building, and weigh as much as an elephant—six tons! The shallow roots of a large Saguaro may spread in a circle up to 100 feet across in order to collect as much water as possible.

WATERY WAKE-UP CALL

Desert wildflowers, such as dune primroses, can "sleep" through 15 years of heat and drought, not sprouting until their wake-up call—a rare, intense desert downpour. Then seeds rush to germinate, flower, and reproduce—all within a few weeks.

NO LEAVES

A tree may lose as much as 600 quarts of water a day through its leaves. Many desert plants, such as Prickly Pears, have no leaves. Instead, they have thick, water-storing stems containing chlorophyll.

*Blooming
Saguaro Cactus
page 71*

Moss Pink

TINY BUT TOUGH

Moss Pink, a member of the carnation family, brightens mountain crevices. It grows in tight, huddled mats to cope with the freezing, drying winds. Its brilliant color stands out against the rocky slopes to attract pollinators.

ALPINE BEAUTIES

Mountains are not all rocky slopes. Hiking a mountain you might find Blue Columbine, the state flower of Colorado, thriving in moist woodlands.

High on a mountain slope

Many mountain flowers are hardy survivors. Growing on rocky slopes above the timberline, they must withstand intense sunlight, cold temperatures, a fierce wind chill factor, thin soil amid rocky rubble, and little rainfall. Most mountain flowers grow in dense cushions or flattened mats.

Blue Columbine

What good are wildflowers?

That depends on your point of view. To most of us, wildflowers are primarily a source of beauty, although they have been used for centuries as herbs, dyes, charms, cosmetics, medicines, and even poisons. We tend to forget that, like all green plants, wildflowers produce the oxygen we need to breathe. Wildflowers also provide food for living things, from the tiniest insect to the largest bear. And all human food comes from plants or plant-eating animals.

WILDFLOWERS THAT HEAL THE EARTH
Some wildflowers, such as alfalfa and clovers, are used by farmers to improve the soil and to feed livestock. A wildflower called Crown Vetch is planted along roadsides to help prevent erosion. All three belong to a group of plants called *legumes*, which harbor bacteria in their roots that improve the soil by replenishing its nitrogen.

Crown Vetch

Alfalfa

Going, going, gone

Wildflowers need our appreciation and conservation efforts if they are to survive. Some are already becoming rare or even endangered due to abuse from humans.

Venus Flytrap page 64

TOO INTRIGUING

The Venus Flytrap is a fascinating plant that is easily dug up and sold for profit. Consequently, it is now classified as an endangered species in both North and South Carolina and is protected by state law in the former.

Trailing Arbutus

TOO DELICATE

Trailing Arbutus is delicate and sensitive to abrupt environmental changes. When roads or houses are built nearby, it almost always disappears right away. It is becoming increasingly uncommon in most areas.

Fringed Gentian page 133

Wild Ginseng page 63

TOO VALUABLE

Ginseng, which should be widespread in North America, is now rare in most areas because it is dug up for its valuable roots.

TOO BEAUTIFUL

Stunningly beautiful wildflowers, such as the blue-violet Fringed Gentian or the luscious pink-and-white Showy Lady's Slipper, are becoming increasingly rare due to overpicking.

43

Using the field guide

T his section features detailed profiles of 50 common North American wildflowers, plus descriptions of over 125 other important species. Color photographs and details about each wildflower are included to help you identify it. Often wildflowers on facing pages are related; sometimes they are not related but look alike or share similar features or habitats. CAUTION labels alert the reader to plants that are poisonous or that cause reactions such as rashes.

Spring Larkspur

Common
St. John
page 88

ICONS

These icons identify a wildflower's general shape and category.

 Hooded Flowers

 Irregular Flowers

Regular Flowers

 Trumpet- & Bell-shaped Flowers

Composite Flowers

Rounded Clusters

Carnivorous Plants

Elongated Clusters

When you go out to look for wildflowers, take a notebook, a pencil, and this field guide or the spotter's guide. Also take a buddy with you. Tell your parents or a grown-up when you are going out. Respect other people's property, and observe the rules for naturalists on page 9 of this guide.

SHAPE ICON

This icon identifies the featured wildflower's general shape and category.

NAME

Each wildflower's common and scientific names appear here.

BOX HEADING

The box heading alerts you to other wildflowers covered in the box that are similar in some way to the main wildflower on the page. These box headings include: Similar Species, In the Same Family, and Look-alikes.

JACK-IN-THE-PULPIT
Arisaema triphyllum

Who's Jack? The name refers to the flower's central club-like spike, which looks somewhat like a preacher standing in an old-fashioned church pulpit.

LOOK FOR: A purple-and-green striped "hood" (*spathe*) protecting a spike at the center (*spadix*).

LEAVES: One or two 3-leaf clusters at the top of long stems that are taller than the pulpit.

HEIGHT: 1–3'

BLOOMS: April–June.

HABITAT: Damp, shady woods and ponds.

RANGE: Eastern and southern regions.

CAUTION: Poisonous.

SIMILAR SPECIES

SKUNK CABBAGE
Symplocarpus foetidus

LOOK FOR: A large, speckled brownish-purple-green spathe around a protruding spike with small flowers. Coiled leaves unfold after flowering, forming dark cabbage-like leaves. The plant's foul-smelling odor attracts pollinating insects. **HEIGHT:** 1–2'. **BLOOMS:** February–May. **HABITAT:** Wet woods, marshes, swamps. **RANGE:** Eastern half of United States, southern Canada.

WATER ARUM
Calla palustris

LOOK FOR: A wide, white spathe surrounding a spike of tiny, yellow flowers and shiny, heart-shaped leaves. **HEIGHT:** 6–12' above water. **BLOOMS:** Late May–August. **HABITAT:** Wetlands. **RANGE:** Northern United States, southeastern Canada.

47

IDENTIFICATION CAPSULE

The identification capsule covers all the details you need to identify a wildflower: color, leaf shape and arrangement, height, blooming time, and other characteristics discussed in Part 2 of this book.

HABITAT AND RANGE

The habitat and range listings tell you whether a wildflower is likely to be found in your part of the country.

Jack-in-the-Pulpit

Arisaema triphyllum

Who's Jack? The name refers to the flower's central club-like spike, which looks somewhat like a preacher standing in an old-fashioned church pulpit.

Look for: A purple-and-green striped "hood" (*spathe*) protecting a spike at the center (*spadix*).

Leaves: One or two 3-leaf clusters at the top of long stems that are taller than the pulpit.

Height: 1–3'.

Blooms: April–June.

Habitat: Damp, shady woods and ponds.

Range: Eastern and southern regions.

Caution: Poisonous.

Skunk Cabbage
Symplocarpus foetidus

Look for: A large, speckled brownish-purple-green spathe around a protruding spike with small flowers. Coiled leaves unfold after flowering, forming dark cabbage-like leaves. The plant's foul-smelling odor attracts pollinating insects.
Height: 1–2'. **Blooms:** February–May.
Habitat: Wet woods, marshes, swamps.
Range: Eastern half of United States, southern Canada.

Water Arum
Calla palustris

Look for: A wide, white spathe surrounding a spike of tiny, yellow flowers and shiny, heart-shaped leaves. **Height:** 6–12" above water. **Blooms:** Late May–August.
Habitat: Wetlands. **Range:** Northern United States, southeastern Canada.

CANADA VIOLET
Viola canadensis

A ren't all violets purple or blue? Guess again! Some are yellow, white, or green-brown. Violets have a second, secret set of flowers: tiny, underground, nonblooming ones that produce seeds by self-pollination. No wonder there are so many of these delicate blossoms!

LOOK FOR: Five white petals with purplish undersides and yellow bases; flower, ¾–1" wide; fragrant; hairy stem.

LEAVES: 2–4" long, heart-shaped, with fine teeth around edges.

HEIGHT: 8–16".

BLOOMS: April–June.

HABITAT: Woods.

RANGE: Northern United States, southern Canada.

STREAM VIOLET
Viola glabella

LOOK FOR: Yellow flowers with purplish lines on lower 3 petals. **HEIGHT:** 2–12". **BLOOMS:** March–July. **HABITAT:** Wet woods. **RANGE:** Western regions.

COMMON BLUE VIOLET
Viola papilionacea

LOOK FOR: Purple, lavender, or white flowers with heart-shaped leaves. **HEIGHT:** 3–8". **BLOOMS:** March–June. **HABITAT:** Damp woods and meadows. **RANGE:** Widespread.

SWEET WHITE VIOLET
Viola blanda

LOOK FOR: White flowers with leaves on separate, reddish stalks. Upper petals bend back. **HEIGHT:** 3–5". **BLOOMS:** April–May. **HABITAT:** Woods. **RANGE:** East to Midwest.

WESTERN PASQUEFLOWER
Anemone occidentalis

BITTERROOT
Lewisia rediviva

LOOK FOR: Pink-to-ivory flowers on short stalks surrounded by clusters of narrow, fleshy, leaves. **HEIGHT:** ½–3".
BLOOMS: May–June. **HABITAT:** Rocky slopes, open sagebrush, pine tree areas.
RANGE: Western regions.

BLOODROOT
Sanguinaria canadensis

LOOK FOR: One white flower with a yellow center; smooth stalk with a palm-shaped leaf. Roots and stem contain red juice. **HEIGHT:** To 10".
BLOOMS: March–May. **HABITAT:** Woods, near streams. **RANGE:** East to Midwest.
CAUTION: Poisonous stem underground.

This flower blooms in early spring, around the time of Easter. In fact, *pasque* is an old French word for Easter. It is sometimes called the Mountain Pasqueflower.

LOOK FOR: A white or cream flower, 1¼–2" wide, at the tip of each very hairy stem. The 5–8 petal-like sepals have fuzzy backs. Each bloom has many stamens.

LEAVES: Narrow, crowded together; growing at the base and also beneath the flower in a circle of 3 leaves; 1½–3" wide.

HEIGHT: 8–24".

BLOOMS: May–September.

HABITAT: Mountain slopes, fields, and meadows.

RANGE: Western regions.

51

STRIPED WINTERGREEN
Chimaphila maculata

BOG WINTERGREEN
Pyrola asarifolia

LOOK FOR: Five to 25 pink flowers hanging from stalk; glossy, tough leaves near base. **HEIGHT:** 6–16". **BLOOMS:** June–September. **HABITAT:** Moist woods. **RANGE:** Widespread.

E asy to identify by its un-usual, white-striped leaves, this plant is used to flavor candy and soda.

LOOK FOR: Drooping, sweet-smelling, white to pink flowers clustered at the tips of the stems; ⅔" wide; 5 petals; 10 stamens.

LEAVES: Long, pointy, ¾–2¾"; evergreen, with vertical, white stripes.

HEIGHT: 3–9".

BLOOMS: June–August.

HABITAT: Woods.

RANGE: East to Midwest.

SHINLEAF
Pyrola elliptica

LOOK FOR: Pink-to-white, smooth, fragrant flowers clustered on stalk; oval leaves at base of stem. **HEIGHT:** 5–10". **BLOOMS:** June–August. **HABITAT:** Woods. **RANGE:** Widespread except West and Southeast.

WOOD NYMPH
Moneses uniflora

LOOK FOR: A solitary white or light pink flower arching from the top of the stem; leaves at base of stem. **HEIGHT:** 2–6". **BLOOMS:** May–August. **HABITAT:** Forests. **RANGE:** Western regions.

53

LARGE-FLOWERED TRILLIUM
Trillium grandiflorum

The name trillium comes from the Latin word for "three." No wonder! This flower has 3 petals, 3 sepals, and 3 leaves!

LOOK FOR: A large flower, 2–4" wide, above a circle of 3 leaves atop a straight stem. The flower has 3 green sepals (not shown in photograph) and 3 wavy-edged, white petals that turn pink as time passes.

LEAVES: Long, 3–6", oval to diamond-shaped, pointed; in whorl of 3. The berries are red.

HEIGHT: 8–18".

BLOOMS: April–June.

HABITAT: Woods.

RANGE: Eastern half of North America.

WESTERN WAKE ROBIN
Trillium ovatum

LOOK FOR: A short plant with 1 white flower above a ring of 3 broad leaves. Rest of stem leafless. **HEIGHT:** 4–16". **BLOOMS:** February–June. **HABITAT:** Stream-banks, woods. **RANGE:** Northwest.

PURPLE TRILLIUM
Trillium erectum

LOOK FOR: Three red petals with 3 green sepals above a ring of 3 diamond-shaped, net-veined leaves. Unpleasant scent. **HEIGHT:** 8–16". **BLOOMS:** April–June. **HABITAT:** Woods. **RANGE:** Most of eastern North America.

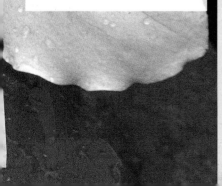

55

FRAGRANT WATER LILY
Nymphaea odorata

The Water Lily isn't a lily at all. It is related to the lotus that ancient Egyptians considered sacred.

LOOK FOR: A sweet-scented floating plant anchored by long stems (rhizomes) in mud. Flowers are 3–5" wide with many white petals and yellow stamens. They stay open until midday only.

LEAVES: Large, 4–12", round, pad-like; shiny green on top, purplish underneath; float on water.

HEIGHT: Up to 8'.

BLOOMS: June–September.

HABITAT: Ponds, lakes.

RANGE: Widespread except West.

INDIAN POND LILY
Nuphar polysepala

LOOK FOR: Heart-shaped, tough leaves floating on water, supporting cup-shaped yellow flowers. **HEIGHT:** Up to 6'. **BLOOMS:** April–September. **HABITAT:** Ponds, quiet streams. **RANGE:** Colorado to southern California, north to Alaska.

AMERICAN LOTUS
Nelumbo lutea

LOOK FOR: A fragrant, pale yellow flower with center that looks a bit like a pepper shaker, on stalks that clear the water. **HEIGHT:** Up to 8'. **BLOOMS:** July–September. **HABITAT:** Ponds and slow streams. **RANGE:** Widespread except West.

OXEYE DAISY
Chrysanthemum leucanthemum

Daisy means "day's eye," and refers to an English daisy that opens only during daylight hours. The Oxeye Daisy, also a native of Europe but now very common here, stays open day and night.

LOOK FOR: A composite flower with white ray flowers surrounding yellow disk flowers; dent in center.

LEAVES: Hunter green, many lobed; lower leaves are longer than upper ones.

HEIGHT: 1–3'.

BLOOMS: May–October.

HABITAT: Prairies, fields.

RANGE: Widespread but less common in the South.

MAYWEED
Anthemis cotula

LOOK FOR: Daisy-like heads; 10–20 rays with dome-like yellow disk. Lacy, bad-smelling leaves. **HEIGHT:** 1–2'. **BLOOMS:** June–October. **HABITAT:** Waste ground. **RANGE:** Widespread.

BLACKFOOT DAISY
Melampodium leucanthum

LOOK FOR: A bushy plant with flower heads of 8–10 broad, white rays around a yellow center. **HEIGHT:** 6–20". **BLOOMS:** March–November. **HABITAT:** Rocky deserts, arid plains. **RANGE:** Southwestern United States.

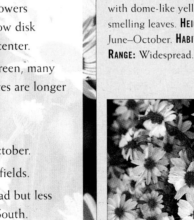

59

INDIAN PIPE
Monotropa uniflora

This ghostly plant, which thrives in deep shade, uses fungi in the soil to break down the nutrients in the roots of decaying plants. Cold and clammy to the touch, it is also called Corpse Plant.

LOOK FOR: Strange, all-white, waxy plant that resembles an upside-down clay pipe. Turns black if picked or touched. One white or pinkish, drooping, bell-shaped flower per stem. Translucent white, thick, and juice-filled stem.

LEAVES: Small scales.

HEIGHT: 10".

BLOOMS: June–September.

HABITAT: Shady woods.

RANGE: Widespread.

SNOW PLANT
Sarcodes sanguinea

LOOK FOR: An entirely red, fleshy plant with bell-shaped flowers and scales for leaves. **HEIGHT:** 8–24". **BLOOMS:** April–July. **HABITAT:** Woods. **RANGE:** Oregon and California.

PINESAP
Monotropa hypopitys

LOOK FOR: A red, pink, lilac, or yellow plant; stem and nodding flowers same color. **HEIGHT:** 4–16". **BLOOMS:** June–November. **HABITAT:** Woods. **RANGE:** Widespread.

ONE-FLOWERED CANCER ROOT
Orobanche uniflora

LOOK FOR: A white to lavender, fragrant flower with yellow center atop stalk. **HEIGHT:** 3–10". **BLOOMS:** April–June. **HABITAT:** Woods. **RANGE:** Widespread.

WILD SARSAPARILLA
Aralia nudicaulis

E arly settlers learned from Native Americans how to use this plant's aromatic roots to brew root beer.

LOOK FOR: A bare stem hiding below a broad, leafy canopy. Tiny, greenish-white flowers with 5 folded-back petals, 5 green stamens, in rounded clusters 1½–2" wide.

LEAVES: Single long leaf stem; 8–15" long, branches into three parts, each with 3–5 oval, toothed leaflets.

HEIGHT: 8–15".

BLOOMS: July–August.

HABITAT: Woods.

RANGE: Widespread except West Coast.

WILD GINSENG
Panax quinquefolium

LOOK FOR: A ball of small white or yellow-green flowers in center of three leaf stems, each with 5 leaflets.
HEIGHT: 8–24".
BLOOMS: May–Aug.
HABITAT: Woods.
RANGE: East to Midwest.

RED BANEBERRY
Actaea rubra

LOOK FOR: Round clusters of creamy white flowers; toothed leaflets. Toxic red fruits.
HEIGHT: 1–2'.
BLOOMS: May–July.
HABITAT: Woods.
RANGE: Widespread, except Southeast.

GOLDENSEAL
Hydrastis canadensis

LOOK FOR: A whitish flower above 2 hand-shaped leaves. No petals; many stamens and pistils.
HEIGHT: 12–16".
BLOOMS: April–May.
HABITAT: Woods.
RANGE: East to Midwest.

The hinged leaves of the Venus Flytrap snap shut on insects that disturb them. Then juices digest the trapped prey. About a week later, the leaves open and the trap is set again.

LOOK FOR: A cluster of white flowers (not shown), each 1" wide; 5 petals; 5 sepals; usually 15 stamens.

LEAVES: At the base of the plant, 1½–6" long; 2 hinged lobes; green on outside, often orange on inside; fringed with spikes.

HEIGHT: 4–12".

BLOOMS: May–June.

HABITAT: Bogs; moist, sandy areas; pinelands.

RANGE: North and South Carolina.

ALERT: Endangered.

NORTHERN PITCHER PLANT
Sarracenia purpurea

LOOK FOR: Red-veined, pitcher-shaped leaves usually half full of water; one purplish-red flower (not shown above) on bare stem. The Northern Pitcher is carnivorous: Its leaves trap, dissolve, and digest insects. **HEIGHT:** 8–24". **BLOOMS:** May–August. **HABITAT:** Bogs. **RANGE:** East to Midwest in United States; Saskatchewan to Nova Scotia.

ROUND-LEAVED SUNDEW
Drosera rotundifolia

LOOK FOR: Round reddish leaves at base, covered with glistening, sweet, sticky hairs that attract and trap insects; cluster of white flowers atop leafless stalk (not shown above). **HEIGHT:** 4–9". **BLOOMS:** June–August. **HABITAT:** Bogs; moist, sandy areas. **RANGE:** Widespread.

65

QUEEN ANNE'S LACE
Daucus carota

Legend explains this lacy white weed's tiny dark red flower as a drop of blood spilled by England's Queen Anne (1665–1714), who pricked her finger making lace. As the plant dies, the flowers curl up to form a "bird's nest." Also called Wild Carrot and Bird's Nest.

LOOK FOR: Tiny white flowers clustered in umbrella shape, about 6" across, usually with tiny reddish-brown flower in the middle (hard to see in photograph); hairy stem.

LEAVES: Fernlike.

HEIGHT: 1–3'.

BLOOMS: May–October.

HABITAT: Fields, roadsides.

RANGE: Widespread.

CAUTION: For some, touching wet leaves may cause a rash.

WATER HEMLOCK
Cicuta maculata

LOOK FOR: Magenta-streaked stem; narrow, notched leaves. **HEIGHT:** 3–6'. **BLOOMS:** June–September. **HABITAT:** Wet meadows, swamps. **RANGE:** East to Midwest. **CAUTION:** Deadly poison.

YARROW
Achillea millefolium

LOOK FOR: Small, white flowers in flat-topped clusters; leaves are fragrant, slender, and shaped like ferns. **HEIGHT:** 1–3'. **BLOOMS:** June–September. **HABITAT:** Fields, roadsides. **RANGE:** Widespread.

COW PARSNIP
Heracleum lanatum

LOOK FOR: A very tall plant with huge, toothed leaves in 3s. **HEIGHT:** 4–9'. **BLOOMS:** April–September. **HABITAT:** Meadows, marshes. **RANGE:** Widespread.

GREAT LAUREL
Rhododendron maximum

This evergreen shrub survives all winter by curling its leaves into tight rolls to conserve heat and moisture.

LOOK FOR: Bunches of white, cup-shaped flowers. Each flower has 5 rounded petals and is 1½–2" wide.

LEAVES: 4–8" long, smooth and pointed. Dark green on top; lighter green and fuzzy underneath. Sticky stem.

HEIGHT: 5–35'.

BLOOMS: June–July.

HABITAT: Damp woodlands.

RANGE: Northeast to Mid-Atlantic regions.

MOUNTAIN LAUREL
Kalmia latifolia

LOOK FOR: A dense evergreen shrub with clusters of dark pink, ribbed buds and pinkish-white flowers. **HEIGHT:** 3–15'. **BLOOMS:** Late May–mid-July. **HABITAT:** Open woods. **RANGE:** Eastern regions. **CAUTION:** Poisonous.

WESTERN AZALEA
Rhododendron occidentale

LOOK FOR: A shrub with large, white-to-pink aromatic flowers; upper lobe with orangish patch; fuzzy stalks. **HEIGHT:** 4–17'. **BLOOMS:** April–August. **HABITAT:** Moist places. **RANGE:** California to Oregon.

69

PRICKLY PEAR
Opuntia humifusa

I f you thought all cacti grew in the desert out west, surprise! This native creeping cactus grows as far east as outer Cape Cod and Nantucket.

LOOK FOR: Yellow, 3"-wide flowers with 12 petals.

LEAVES: None; stems are flat, fleshy pads with tiny stinging bristles.

HEIGHT: 1'.

BLOOMS: May–August.

HABITAT: Dunes, sandy places.

RANGE: Eastern regions.

TEDDYBEAR CHOLLA
Opuntia bigelovii

LOOK FOR: A tree-like stem with stubby branches covered with barbed spines; flowers yellow or green. **HEIGHT:** 3–9'.
BLOOMS: May–June.
HABITAT: Deserts.
RANGE: California to Arizona.

BARREL CACTUS
Ferocactus acanthodes

LOOK FOR: A single barrel-shaped stem with reddish or yellowish spines; crown of reddish flowers.
HEIGHT: 3–10'.
BLOOMS: April–May.
HABITAT: Deserts.
RANGE: Southwest.

SAGUARO
Cereus gigantea

LOOK FOR: White clusters of flowers atop gigantic, spiny stems, some taller than a house.
HEIGHT: Up to 50'.
BLOOMS: May–June.
HABITAT: Deserts.
RANGE: California to Arizona.

COMMON BUTTERCUP
Ranunculus acris

E volution hasn't altered the structure of the buttercup, one of our most successful flowers. Its wide-open, shiny, yellow petals make the buttercup easily accessible to pollinating bees, flies, wasps, and beetles.

LOOK FOR: An upright, hairy plant with 1"-wide, golden-yellow flowers; 5 glossy, overlapping petals; 5 shorter, greenish, spreading sepals; many pistils and bushy stamens.

LEAVES: 1–4" wide on long stalk, divided into 5–7 toothed leaflets.

HEIGHT: 2–3'.

BLOOMS: May–September.

HABITAT: Fields, meadows.

RANGE: Widespread.

CAUTION: Contains a toxic juice that can cause blisters and stomach upsets.

MARSH MARIGOLD
Caltha palustris
LOOK FOR: Large, heart-shaped leaves; thick succulent stem; oversized buttercup flowers. **HEIGHT:** 1–2'. **BLOOMS:** April–June. **HABITAT:** Streams, swamps. **RANGE:** Canada, eastern United States.

SAGEBRUSH BUTTERCUP
Ranunculus glaberrimus
LOOK FOR: 5–8 shiny, yellow petals on small, fleshy plant. **HEIGHT:** 2–8". **BLOOMS:** March–June. **HABITAT:** Sagebrush steppes, pine forests. **RANGE:** Western regions.

RUE ANEMONE
Anemonella thalictroides
LOOK FOR: 2–3 white or pink flowers (sepals, not petals) above whorl of 3 round-lobed leaflets. **HEIGHT:** 4–8". **BLOOMS:** April–May. **HABITAT:** Woods. **RANGE:** East to central United States.

73

CANADA LILY
Lilium canadense

The lily family numbers thousands of species, but all have one thing in common. Their flower parts—petals, sepals, and stamens—come in multiples of 3.

LOOK FOR: One or more nodding flowers per stalk, up to 16–20 per plant; 2–3" wide. Yellow to dark orange, with reddish-brown spots. 3 petals, 3 petal-like sepals, all arching; 6 stamens with brown anthers.

LEAVES: Up to 6" long; lance-shaped; in whorls of 4–10; prickly veins on underside.

HEIGHT: 2–5'.

BLOOMS: June–August.

HABITAT: Woods, wet meadows.

RANGE: East to Midwest.

TIGER LILY
Lilium columbianum

LOOK FOR: Large, orange, bell-like flowers with petals curled back, spotted with red and purple. **HEIGHT:** 2–4'. **BLOOMS:** May–August. **HABITAT:** Prairies, forests. **RANGE:** Northwest.

WOOD LILY
Lilium philadelphicum

LOOK FOR: 1–5 red, funnel-shaped flowers with yellowish, purple-speckled bases. **HEIGHT:** 12–28". **BLOOMS:** June–August. **HABITAT:** Meadows, forests. **RANGE:** Widespread.

YELLOW FAWN LILY
Erythronium grandiflorum

LOOK FOR: 1–5 pale to bright yellow flowers per stalk. **HEIGHT:** 6–12". **BLOOMS:** March–August. **HABITAT:** Sagebrush slopes, mountain forests. **RANGE:** Northwest.

75

COMMON SUNFLOWER
Helianthus annuus

Greek myth tells of a water nymph who fell in love with the sun god Apollo and spent every hour gazing at the sun until she turned into a sunflower. A sunflower does turn its head to follow the sun.

LOOK FOR: Yellow ray flowers around central reddish-brown disk flowers. Branching stems. Sharp, bristly hairs on all green parts.

LEAVES: Long, toothed, rough, heart-shaped.

HEIGHT: 2–12'.

BLOOMS: June–November.

HABITAT: Fields, prairies, roadsides.

RANGE: Widespread.

BLACK-EYED SUSAN
Rudbeckia hirta

LOOK FOR: Yellow ray flowers around central brown disk flowers that form a cone; hairy leaves. **HEIGHT:** 1–3'. **BLOOMS:** June–October. **HABITAT:** Fields, prairies, woods. **RANGE:** Widespread.

JERUSALEM ARTICHOKE
Helianthus tuberosus

LOOK FOR: Yellow ray flowers around central yellow disk flowers; thick, rough, toothed leaves. **HEIGHT:** 5–10'. **BLOOMS:** August–October. **HABITAT:** Moist soil. **RANGE:** Widespread.

ARROWLEAF BALSAM ROOT
Balsamorhiza sagittata

LOOK FOR: A single yellow flower; large, silvery-gray, fuzzy leaves at base. **HEIGHT:** 8–32". **BLOOMS:** May–July. **HABITAT:** Grasslands, sagebrush, pine forests. **RANGE:** Western regions.

COMMON DANDELION
Taraxacum officinale

The name Dandelion comes from the French *dent de lion*, or "tooth of the lion." It refers to the plant's large, jagged, tooth-edged leaves. After blooming, the yellow flowers turn into fluffy white blowballs, each with hundreds of seeds that are swept away on the wind.

LOOK FOR: One yellow flower head atop stalk; "petals" are tiny, individual ray flowers; white, fluffy blowball with hundreds of seeds, each with its own little "parachute." Stem contains milky sap.

LEAVES: Toothed leaves clustered at base.

HEIGHT: 2–18".

BLOOMS: March–September.

HABITAT: Lawns, fields, roadsides.

RANGE: Widespread.

YELLOW GOATSBEARD
Tragopogon dubius

LOOK FOR: A pale yellow flower head (all ray flowers) with bracts extending past flower tips. Hollow stems; huge fluffy blowball; milky sap; a few grass-like leaves. **HEIGHT:** 16–32". **BLOOMS:** May–September. **HABITAT:** Roadsides, fields. **RANGE:** Widespread.

DESERT DANDELION
Malacothrix glabrata

LOOK FOR: Butter-colored flower heads (all ray flowers) on branched stems with feathery leaves (most near base). **HEIGHT:** 6–14". **BLOOMS:** March–June. **HABITAT:** Sandy deserts, plains. **RANGE:** Parts of Idaho, Oregon, California, Arizona.

79

YELLOW LADY'S SLIPPER
Cypripedium calceolus

The species name for this flower (*calceolus*) comes from a Latin term meaning "a little shoe." Also called moccasin flower, this plant was used by Native Americans to treat toothaches.

LOOK FOR: A fragrant flower with one yellow, pouch-like, slipper-shaped petal, 1–2" long; 2 greenish-yellow to brownish-purple side petals that twist into a spiral; and 2 greenish-yellow, lance-shaped sepals.

LEAVES: Up to 8" long with veins running parallel; hairy stem, often twisted.

HEIGHT: 4–28".

BLOOMS: April–August.

HABITAT: Bogs, swamps, woods.

RANGE: Widespread.

CAUTION: Tiny hairs can cause rash.

PINK LADY'S SLIPPER

Cypripedium acaule

LOOK FOR: A petal that is pink, pouch-like, veined, grooved on front; other petals and sepals greenish-brown. **HEIGHT:** 6–15". **BLOOMS:** April–July. **HABITAT:** Woods. **RANGE:** East to Midwest.

MOUNTAIN LADY'S SLIPPER

Cypripedium montanum

LOOK FOR: One slipper-shaped petal; other petals and sepals dark purple, twisted. **HEIGHT:** 8–28". **BLOOMS:** May–July. **HABITAT:** Wooded valleys. **RANGE:** Northwest.

SHOWY LADY'S SLIPPER

Cypripedium reginae

LOOK FOR: One white-and-pink, slipper-like, veined petal; other petals and sepals white. **HEIGHT:** 1–3'. **BLOOMS:** May–August. **HABITAT:** Woods, bogs. **RANGE:** East but not Southeast.

81

CANADA GOLDENROD
Solidago canadensis

Long blamed for the miseries of allergy sufferers, goldenrod is unjustly accused. The real culprit is ragweed. Many bees and butterflies visit goldenrods for their nectar.

LOOK FOR: Arrowhead-shaped clusters of tiny yellow blooms on tall, wand-like stems.

LEAVES: Up to 5", lance-shaped, toothed, hairy leaves with 3 major veins. Stem is finely hairy.

HEIGHT: 1–5'.

BLOOMS: August–October.

HABITAT: Fields, open woods, roadsides.

RANGE: Southeastern Canada to eastern United States.

LANCE-LEAVED GOLDENROD
Solidago graminifolia

LOOK FOR: Clusters of small, yellow flowers with narrow, pointed leaves and branching stems. **HEIGHT:** 2–4'. **BLOOMS:** July–October. **HABITAT:** Along roads and in dense underbrush. **RANGE:** Southern Canada; east, south to North Carolina; Northwest.

SEASIDE GOLDENROD
Solidago sempervirens

LOOK FOR: Delicate bunches of large, yellow flowers on arching branches; succulent leaves. **HEIGHT:** 1–8'. **BLOOMS:** August–November. **HABITAT:** Salt marshes, sandy sites. **RANGE:** East Coast; west along Gulf Coast to Texas.

BLACK MUSTARD
Brassica nigra

Like mustard on your hot dog? It comes from the seeds of this European import —a relative of broccoli, cauliflower, and brussels sprouts!

LOOK FOR: Crowded clusters of small, yellow flowers near tops of stems, on widely branching plant.

LEAVES: Lower leaves are lobed and bristly; upper leaves are smaller, lance-shaped, hairless.

HEIGHT: 2–3', sometimes to 12'.

BLOOMS: June–October.

HABITAT: Fields, vacant lots.

RANGE: Widespread but rare in Southeast.

CHARLOCK
Brassica kaber

LOOK FOR: A fuzzy, leafy plant with many yellow flowers at tips of branches.
HEIGHT: 1–3'. **BLOOMS:** January–June.
HABITAT: Fields, roadsides, vacant lots.
RANGE: Widespread.

PLAINS WALL-FLOWER
Erysimum asperum

LOOK FOR: A short stem, branched near top with clusters of yellow flowers; narrow leaves. **HEIGHT:** 6–14". **BLOOMS:** April–July. **HABITAT:** Plains. **RANGE:** East of the Rockies.

COMMON WINTER CRESS
Barbarea vulgaris

LOOK FOR: Yellow flower clusters, unusual 5-part leaves with end leaf larger and rounder than other 4. **HEIGHT:** 1–2'. **BLOOMS:** April–August. **HABITAT:** Fields, meadows. **RANGE:** East, Midwest.

R abbits, deer, and other mammals feed on this shrub that Navajo Indians used to make a yellow dye. The Latin species name describes the sickening odor of its leaves.

LOOK FOR: Clusters of small, yellow, star-like flowers, ¼–½".

LEAVES: Narrow, covered with white hairs; ¾–3" long. Stem erect, slender, flexible; stem and branches covered with white, woolly hairs.

HEIGHT: Up to 7'.

BLOOMS: August–October.

HABITAT: Deserts, grasslands, open woods.

RANGE: Western regions.

BRITTLEBUSH
Encelia farinosa

LOOK FOR: A round, leafy bush with brilliant yellow flowers and hairy, oval leaves. Fragrant resin in stems.
HEIGHT: 3–5'. **BLOOMS:** March–June.
HABITAT: Deserts.
RANGE: Southwest.

GIANT COREOPSIS
Coreopsis gigantea

LOOK FOR: Yellow flowers and feathery leaves atop a soft, woody, tree-like stem. **HEIGHT:** 1–10'. **BLOOMS:** March–May.
HABITAT: Coastal dunes. **RANGE:** California.

SNAKEWEED
Gutierrezia sarothrae

LOOK FOR: A small, round shrub with numerous tiny, yellow flowers.
HEIGHT: 6–36".
BLOOMS: August–September. **HABITAT:** Deserts, plains.
RANGE: Western regions to central Canada.

This European weed was so named because it blooms about the same time as the festival of St. John the Baptist (June 24th) in England. It is called Klamath Weed in the West.

LOOK FOR: Yellow flowers with 5 petals in a star-like formation, with black dots on some petal tips; many long stamens.

LEAVES: 1–2" long with black see-through dots; paired; oval.

HEIGHT: 1–2½'.

BLOOMS: June–August.

HABITAT: Along roads, open fields, waste grounds.

RANGE: Widespread.

CAUTION: Poisonous.

ST. PETERSWORT
Hypericum stans

LOOK FOR: Yellow flowers; 4, not 5, petals; no dots; many stamens.
HEIGHT: 1–3'. **BLOOMS:** July–September.
HABITAT: Sandy areas. **RANGE:** East, South, central states.

TINKER'S PENNY
Hypericum anagalloides

LOOK FOR: A leafy mat of small yellow flowers (5 petals) that grow along the ground. **HEIGHT:** Creeper, stems to 8".
BLOOMS: June–August. **HABITAT:** Wet places. **RANGE:** Western regions.

89

EVENING PRIMROSE
Oenothera biennis

BIRDCAGE EVENING PRIMROSE
Oenothera deltoides

LOOK FOR: A grayish plant that grows along a surface; large, white, fluffy flowers and drooping buds; circle of leaves at plant's base. **HEIGHT:** Creeper, stems 4–40" long. **BLOOMS:** March–May. **HABITAT:** Dry, sandy areas. **RANGE:** Oregon, California, Arizona, Utah.

HOOKER'S EVENING PRIMROSE
Oenothera hookeri

LOOK FOR: A tall, upright stem with large yellow flowers, 4 reddish sepals, and long, narrow, alternate leaves. **HEIGHT:** 2–3'. **BLOOMS:** June–September. **HABITAT:** Along roads, on hillsides, in grassy fields. **RANGE:** Western regions.

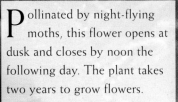

Pollinated by night-flying moths, this flower opens at dusk and closes by noon the following day. The plant takes two years to grow flowers.

LOOK FOR: Large (1–2" wide) lemon-scented, yellow flowers atop leafy stalks; 4 broad petals; 4 sepals bent backward; an X-shaped stigma.

LEAVES: 4–8" long, in pairs; rough, hairy, pointy; slightly toothed. Stem hairy, light red-purple.

HEIGHT: 2–5'.

BLOOMS: June–September.

HABITAT: Sandy fields, roadsides.

RANGE: Widespread.

91

BIRDSFOOT TREFOIL
Lotus corniculatus

This wildflower's name refers to its slender, spread-out seedpods that look like a bird's foot.

Look for: Low-to-the-ground clusters of yellow flowers (½" wide) that redden as they age; 5 petals.

Leaves: Leaflets in 5s (3 at tip of stalk, 2 at base).

Height: Creeper; stems 6–24" long, sometimes erect at tips.

Blooms: May–September.

Habitat: Fields, roadsides.

Range: Widespread.

Wild Indigo
Baptisia tinctoria

Look for: Many clusters of yellow flowers; leaflets oval, in 3s, scattered on stem. **Height:** 3'. **Blooms:** May–September. **Habitat:** Dry fields. **Range:** East to central regions.

Silky Beach Pea
Lathyrus littoralis

Look for: A hairy, gray plant in low patches with purplish-pink flowers; leaves in pairs. **Height:** 8–24". **Blooms:** April–June. **Habitat:** Dunes. **Range:** Pacific Coast.

93

CALIFORNIA POPPY
Eschscholtzia californica

Poppies can turn a hillside ablaze with color, but their petals close when the clouds roll in and when the sun goes down. Their spicy scent attracts beetles, which pollinate the flowers.

LOOK FOR: Bright orange to golden yellow, cup-shaped flowers (1–2" wide) with 4 large, fan-like petals; one flower per stem.

LEAVES: Fern-shaped, bluish-green.

HEIGHT: 8–24".

BLOOMS: February–September.

HABITAT: Grassy areas, roadsides.

RANGE: Far West.

CAUTION: Poisonous.

PRICKLY POPPY
Argemone polyanthemos

LOOK FOR: White, wrinkled petals, center cluster of yellow stamens; prickles all over. **HEIGHT:** Up to 4'. **BLOOMS:** April–July. **HABITAT:** Plains. **RANGE:** South Dakota south to New Mexico. **CAUTION:** Poisonous.

DESERT ROSE MALLOW
Hibiscus coulteri

LOOK FOR: Large, cup-shaped, cream-to-yellow flowers, commonly tinged with red; rough hairs. **HEIGHT:** Up to 4'. **BLOOMS:** Year-round in warm places. **HABITAT:** Deserts. **RANGE:** Arizona to Texas.

WOOD POPPY
Stylophorum diphyllum

LOOK FOR: Yellow flowers with one pair of lobed leaves on stem. **HEIGHT:** 1–1½'. **BLOOMS:** March–May. **HABITAT:** Woods. **RANGE:** Mid-Atlantic to Midwest.

Northwest Native Americans made chewing gum from hawkweed. The plant's name comes from an old belief that hawks ate the weed to improve their eyesight. Also called Devil's Paintbrush.

Look for: Fiery orange flowers (¾" wide); toothed rays atop a hairy, leafless stalk. Green leaves around flowers (bracts) are covered with black hairs.

Leaves: Long (2–5"), hairy, clustered at base.

Height: 1–2'.

Blooms: June–August.

Habitat: Fields, roadsides.

Range: Northeast to Mid-Atlantic to Midwest.

Two-flowered Cynthia
Krigia biflora

Look for: Yellow-orange flowers, twice as big as Orange Hawkweed; 1–2 small, oval leaves are below fork in stem.
Height: 1–2'. **Blooms:** May–August.
Habitat: Open woodlands and fields.
Range: Eastern regions to Missouri.

Yellow Hawkweed
Hieracium pratense

Look for: A plant similar to Orange Hawkweed, except for yellow flower color. **Height:** 1–3'. **Blooms:** May–August. **Habitat:** Pastures, roadsides. **Range:** East; south to Georgia; west to Tennessee.

97

BUTTERFLY WEED
Asclepias tuberosa

A favorite of butterflies, this plant has thin, watery sap, unlike the milkier sap of most other milkweeds. Native Americans used the fibers of this plant to make bowstrings.

LOOK FOR: Small, star-shaped, bright orange flowers (⅜") in 2"-wide clusters.

LEAVES: Narrow, oval-shaped; 2–6" long. Stem leafy; fuzzy.

HEIGHT: 1–2½'.

BLOOMS: June–September.

HABITAT: Fields, roadsides.

RANGE: Widespread except far West.

CAUTION: Some plants in the Milkweed family are poisonous.

SHOWY MILKWEED
Asclepias speciosa

LOOK FOR: Umbrella-like clusters of pinkish, star-shaped flowers on pale green plants. Milky sap. **HEIGHT:** 1–4'. **BLOOMS:** May–August. **HABITAT:** Brush, open forests. **RANGE:** Western to central United States.

COMMON MILKWEED
Asclepias syriaca

LOOK FOR: Purplish-pink, star-shaped flower clusters; milky sap; warty seedpods. **HEIGHT:** 2–6'. **BLOOMS:** June–August. **HABITAT:** Fields, roads. **RANGE:** East to Midwest.

SWAMP MILKWEED
Asclepias incarnata

LOOK FOR: Smaller flowers and narrower leaves than those of Common Milkweed. **HEIGHT:** 1–4'. **BLOOMS:** June–August. **HABITAT:** Swamps, shores. **RANGE:** Widespread except West.

GIANT RED PAINTBRUSH
Castilleja miniata

These tall, red-tipped flowers offer no landing areas for bees. Instead, they rely on hummingbirds and hovering insects for pollination.

LOOK FOR: Clusters of red-tipped, tube-shaped flowers, ¾–1½" long, atop straight stems.

LEAVES: 4" long; lance-shaped; alternate. Leaves just below flowers (bracts) are red with 3 pointed lobes.

HEIGHT: 1–3'.

BLOOMS: May–September.

HABITAT: Mountain meadows, open forests.

RANGE: Widespread.

INDIAN PAINTBRUSH
(PAINTED CUP) *Castilleja coccinea*

LOOK FOR: Red-tipped, fan-like leaves at base of flower (bracts) nearly hide the greenish-yellow flower inside; finger-like leaves along stem. **HEIGHT:** 1–2'. **BLOOMS:** May–July. **HABITAT:** Meadows, prairies. **RANGE:** East to central North America.

DESERT PAINTBRUSH
Castilleja chromosa

LOOK FOR: Brilliant, orange-red, flower-like tips on straight stem; leaves at flower's base (bracts) also red. Leaves are narrow. **HEIGHT:** 4–16". **BLOOMS:** April–August. **HABITAT:** Dry, open areas. **RANGE:** Western United States.

101

CARDINAL FLOWER
Lobelia cardinalis

This bright red beauty, named for the robes of Roman Catholic cardinals, is a favorite of hummingbirds and hikers alike. Unfortunately, it is becoming more scarce due to overpicking.

LOOK FOR: A tall spire (up to 20") of scarlet flowers atop a vertical stalk. Flowers have 2 upper and 3 lower petals.

LEAVES: Spear-shaped, toothed.

HEIGHT: Up to 4'.

BLOOMS: July–September.

HABITAT: Wooded streambanks, wet meadows.

RANGE: East to central regions; Southwest.

SALVIA
Salvia coccinea

LOOK FOR: Clusters of red flowers, widely spaced on square stem; heart-shaped leaves.
HEIGHT: 1–2'.
BLOOMS: May–frost.
HABITAT: Sandy soil.
RANGE: Southeast and central regions.

SCARLET BUGLER
Penstemon centranthifolius

LOOK FOR: Red, tube-shaped flowers in narrow spires; lance-shaped leaves.
HEIGHT: 1–4'.
BLOOMS: April–July.
HABITAT: Brush.
RANGE: Coastal mountains of California.

TEXAS BETONY
Stachys coccinea

LOOK FOR: A plant similar to Salvia but hairy and with more flowers in spike atop stem. **HEIGHT:** Up to 3'. **BLOOMS:** March–October. **HABITAT:** Rock crevices on slopes. **RANGE:** Southwest.

TRUMPET HONEYSUCKLE
Lonicera sempervirens

Hummingbirds are attracted to the strong, sweet scent and bright red blooms of this climbing, woody vine. The tubelike flowers are so deep, the plant relies exclusively on hummingbirds for pollination.

LOOK FOR: A vine with groups of trumpet-shaped flowers (1–2" long) that are red outside, yellow inside.

LEAVES: Pairs of leaves meet at their bases so that the stem seems to go through them like a straw.

HEIGHT: Climbing vine.

BLOOMS: April–September.

HABITAT: Woods, brush-covered areas.

RANGE: Eastern and central regions.

JAPANESE HONEYSUCKLE
Lonicera japonica

LOOK FOR: A fragrant, climbing vine with white, tube-shaped flowers (yellowing with age), with petals bending backward, revealing long stamens. Leaves are in pairs, evergreen, and fuzzy. **HEIGHT:** Vine. **BLOOMS:** April–July. **HABITAT:** Woods, thickets. **RANGE:** East to southern-central regions.

NORTHERN BUSH HONEYSUCKLE
Diervilla lonicera

LOOK FOR: A low shrub with yellow, tube-shaped flowers and toothed, stalked leaves. **HEIGHT:** 4–5'. **BLOOMS:** June–August. **HABITAT:** Woods. **RANGE:** Southern states.

105

This plant is also known as Crane's Bill because of its beak-like seedpods. When mature, the pods burst, flinging seeds as far as 22 feet away.

LOOK FOR: A hairy plant with several stems and bright pink to purple flowers (1" wide) in branched clusters near top of stems. 5 petals; 10 stamens.

LEAVES: Wide, toothed, with 5–7 lobes, most near base.

HEIGHT: 1–3'.

BLOOMS: May–August.

HABITAT: Meadows, open forests.

RANGE: Western regions.

WILD GERANIUM
Geranium maculatum

LOOK FOR: Lavender-to-rose flowers in bunches of 2–5, above a pair of gray-green leaves. **HEIGHT:** 1–2'.
BLOOMS: April–June. **HABITAT:** Woods, meadows. **RANGE:** Eastern and central North America.

HERB ROBERT
Geranium robertianum

LOOK FOR: Pink-to-purplish flowers are smaller than those of Sticky and Wild Geraniums; fuzzy, reddish stems; unpleasant odor. **HEIGHT:** 1–2'. **BLOOMS:** May–October. **HABITAT:** Rocky woods. **RANGE:** Eastern and central North America, excluding Southeast.

107

RED MAIDS
Calandrinia ciliata

This West Coast wildflower produces shiny black seeds, a favorite food of birds and rodents. Its scientific name is a tribute to an 18th-century Swiss botanist, J. L. Calandrini.

LOOK FOR: Brilliant red to pink flowers with pale, star-like centers, 5 petals, and 2 hairy sepals. The flowers bloom for just one day.

LEAVES: Long, lance-shaped leaves around base; shorter ones above. Leaves are succulent (fleshy for storing water), and fringed with hairs. Several stems, 2–16" long.

HEIGHT: Under 6".

BLOOMS: April–May.

HABITAT: Weedy fields, moist gravel.

RANGE: West and Southwest.

ROSE MOSS (ROSE PURSLANE)
Portulaca pilosa

LOOK FOR: A low, branching plant with small rosy flowers (many yellow stamens); tufts of white hair on stem. **HEIGHT:** 2–8". **BLOOMS:** June–October. **HABITAT:** Sandy soil. **RANGE:** Southeast and Gulf Coast states.

MOSS CAMPION
Silene acaulis

LOOK FOR: A mossy carpet of pink-to-violet flowers, each with 5 petals at the end of leafy branch. **HEIGHT:** 1–3". **BLOOMS:** June–August. **HABITAT:** Mountaintops. **RANGE:** Arctic, West, Northeast.

VIOLET WOOD SORREL
Oxalis violacea

LOOK FOR: Rose-purple flowers with heart-shaped leaves in 3s, purplish underneath. **HEIGHT:** 4–8". **BLOOMS:** April–June. **HABITAT:** Open woods, prairies. **RANGE:** East to Midwest; Southwest.

SWAMP ROSE MALLOW
Hibiscus palustris

Unusual stamens identify members of the mallow family: They form a column around the style. This plant was not used to make marshmallows, but the roots of its relative—the Marsh Mallow—were!

LOOK FOR: A pink, very wide (4–7") flower with stamens and style forming a yellowish column. Musky scent.

LEAVES: Yellow-green, 4" long, oval, toothed with white fuzz underneath; arranged alternately on stem.

HEIGHT: 3–8'.

BLOOMS: July–September.

HABITAT: Marshes, streambanks.

RANGE: East, Southeast, Midwest.

CORN COCKLE
Agrostemma githago

LOOK FOR: A very hairy plant with pink flowers atop long stalks; 5 sepals extend beyond the 5 petals; leaves are long, narrow, in pairs. **HEIGHT:** 1–3'. **BLOOMS:** June–September. **HABITAT:** Wheat fields and waste grounds. **RANGE:** Widespread. **CAUTION:** Seeds are poisonous.

MUSK MALLOW
Malva moschata

LOOK FOR: Pink (or white or lavender) flowers with 5 wedge-shaped petals; musk-scented; leaves divided into several toothed lobes. **HEIGHT:** 8–24". **BLOOMS:** June–October. **HABITAT:** Roadsides, fields, empty lots. **RANGE:** East and Mid-Atlantic to central states.

111

DEPTFORD PINK
Dianthus armeria

These flowers were not named for their color, but rather for the pinked—or saw-toothed—edges of their petals. In fact, the name of the color pink came from these flowers.

Look for: Small, deep pink, white-spotted flowers (½" wide) clustered atop stiff, vertical stems; 5 petals; long bristly leaves below flowers (bracts).

Leaves: 1–4", narrow, erect.

Height: 6–24".

Blooms: May–September.

Habitat: Fields, roadsides.

Range: Widespread.

FIRE PINK
Silene virginica

Look for: Bright red flowers with 5 narrow, notched petals; oval, hairy leaves. **Height:** 6–24". **Blooms:** April–June. **Habitat:** Open woods, slopes. **Range:** Eastern to central regions.

SALT-MARSH PINK
Sabatia stellaris

Look for: Pink flowers with yellowish, star-like center, with red outline. **Height:** 6–18". **Blooms:** July–October. **Habitat:** Marshes, meadows. **Range:** East Coast and Gulf Coast states.

CHICKWEED
Stellaria media

Look for: A low plant; 5 petals split so they look like 10; 5 green sepals longer than petals. **Height:** 3–8". **Blooms:** February–December. **Habitat:** Lawns, empty lots. **Range:** Widespread.

NEW ENGLAND ASTER
Aster novae-angliae

Despite its name, this late-bloomer isn't limited to New England, but can be found in much of the East and Midwest. The word *aster* is Greek for "star."

LOOK FOR: 40–100 lavender to purplish-blue ray flowers surrounding yellow disk flowers; heads: 1–2" wide.

LEAVES: Long (1½–5") and lance-shaped, they seem to clasp the sticky, hairy stem.

HEIGHT: 3–7'.

BLOOMS: August–October.

HABITAT: Wet fields and swampy areas.

RANGE: Across southern Canada; eastern and midwestern United States.

COMMON FLEABANE
Erigeron philadelphicus

LOOK FOR: Many small, white-to-pink ray flowers around a yellow disk. Leaves seem to clasp stem. **HEIGHT:** 6–36". **BLOOMS:** May–August. **HABITAT:** Fields, woods. **RANGE:** Widespread.

SEASIDE DAISY
Erigeron glaucous

LOOK FOR: Low-growing flowers with light pink to lavender rays around yellow disk; sticky stems. **HEIGHT:** 4–16". **BLOOMS:** April–August. **HABITAT:** Coasts. **RANGE:** Pacific Coast.

STICKY ASTER
Machaeranthera bigelovii

LOOK FOR: Reddish-purple rays; yellow disk; spiny leaves. **HEIGHT:** 1–3'. **BLOOMS:** August–October. **HABITAT:** Plains, coniferous forests. **RANGE:** New Mexico, Colorado, Arizona.

BULL THISTLE
Cirsium vulgare

Famous for their armor of prickly spines and aggressive takeovers of fields and farms, thistles have been cut down, dug up, and even outlawed in 37 states! Bees use them to produce a fine honey.

LOOK FOR: Bristly, rose-purple disk flowers (no ray flowers) enclosed by a spiny, cup-shaped base of yellow-tipped leaves under flowers (bracts); spiny stems.

LEAVES: Narrow with spines at tips.

HEIGHT: 2–6'.

BLOOMS: July–September.

HABITAT: Fields, roadsides.

RANGE: Widespread.

COMMON BURDOCK
Arctium minus

LOOK FOR: A bushy plant with pink-to-lavender flower heads; prickly ball of bracts; large leaves. **HEIGHT:** 1–5'. **BLOOMS:** July–October. **HABITAT:** Fields. **RANGE:** Widespread except Northwest.

YELLOW THISTLE
Cirsium horridulum

LOOK FOR: Large, yellow flowers with spiny leaves that seem to clasp the stem. **HEIGHT:** 1–5'. **BLOOMS:** May–August. **HABITAT:** Shores, marshes, fields. **RANGE:** East of the Rockies.

SPOTTED KNAPWEED
Centaurea maculosa

LOOK FOR: Purple disk flowers atop spiky black-tipped leaves under flowers (bracts). **HEIGHT:** 2–3'. **BLOOMS:** June–August. **HABITAT:** Fields, roadsides, lots. **RANGE:** Widespread.

117

WILD BERGAMOT
Monarda fistulosa

The fragrant leaves of this plant, a member of the mint family, have been used to brew tea.

LOOK FOR: Clusters of lavender, tube-shaped flowers, each 1" long; hairy, lower petals bend backward.

LEAVES: About 2½" long; gray-green, in pairs, spear-shaped, toothed. Stem: square.

HEIGHT: 2–4'.

BLOOMS: June–September.

HABITAT: Dry fields, prairies, thickets.

RANGE: Eastern North America.

CATNIP
Nepeta cataria

LOOK FOR: Purple spots on white-lilac, tube-shaped flowers; stem and leaves have soft, white hairs. **HEIGHT:** 1–3'. **BLOOMS:** June–September. **HABITAT:** Roadsides, pastures. **RANGE:** Widespread.

FIELD MINT
Mentha arvensis

LOOK FOR: Tiny, lavender or white flowers around a squarish stem; aromatic leaves. **HEIGHT:** 6–24". **BLOOMS:** July–September. **HABITAT:** Wet places. **RANGE:** Widespread.

DESERT SAGE
Salvia dorrii

LOOK FOR: A bush with spine-tipped branches, gray-green leaves, and brilliant blue flowers. **HEIGHT:** 8–32". **BLOOMS:** May–July. **HABITAT:** Dry areas. **RANGE:** West.

RED CLOVER
Trifolium pratense

I mported from Europe and planted here as a hay crop, this plant improves the soil and has long been considered a good luck omen, especially the rare four-leaf clover.

LOOK FOR: A sweet-smelling mass of tiny magenta flowers; one big flower head atop each hairy stem.

LEAVES: A pale, wide V appears on the oval leaflets, which are in groups of three.

HEIGHT: 6–24".

BLOOMS: May–September.

HABITAT: Open areas.

RANGE: Widespread.

SILVERLEAF LOCOWEED
Oxytropis sericea

LOOK FOR: A spike of white or cream flowers on long stalk. **HEIGHT:** 3–16". **BLOOMS:** May–September. **HABITAT:** Prairies, mountains. **RANGE:** Rocky Mountains area. **CAUTION:** Poisonous.

BIGHEAD CLOVER
Trifolium macrocephalum

LOOK FOR: A low plant with large round heads of 2-toned red, pea-like flowers. **HEIGHT:** 4–12". **BLOOMS:** April–June. **HABITAT:** Meadows. **RANGE:** Northwest.

FIELD MILKWORT
Polygala sanguinea

LOOK FOR: Tiny rose-pink flowers in tube-shaped, head-like clusters; narrow leaves. **HEIGHT:** 5–15". **BLOOMS:** June–October. **HABITAT:** Grasslands. **RANGE:** East to central states.

121

LARGE PURPLE FRINGED ORCHID
Habenaria fimbriata

This orchid holds pollen in a little sac (botanists call it a spur) that sticks to moths and butterflies when they fly off to the next flower, ensuring that pollination occurs.

Look for: Fringed, fragrant, lavender flowers in a long cluster. The lower lip of each flower has three fan-shaped lobes and a spur that points backward.

Leaves: Long (8"), lance-shaped at base; stem leaves smaller.

Height: 2–4'.

Blooms: June–August.

Habitat: Wet woods, meadows, swamps.

Range: Northeast to Mid-Atlantic regions.

HOODED LADIES' TRESSES
Spiranthes romanzoffiana

Look for: A spike with up to 60 white flowers in 1–4 spiraled rows; 3–6 lance-shaped leaves at base. **Height:** 4–24". **Blooms:** July–October. **Habitat:** Moist, open places. **Range:** Northern and southwestern North America.

YELLOW FRINGED ORCHID
Habenaria ciliaris

Look for: A cluster of orange-to-yellow flowers with nodding, fringed lip petals atop stem. **Height:** 1–2½'. **Blooms:** July–September. **Habitat:** Wet, sandy woods; meadows. **Range:** East (except New England) to Midwest and Texas.

123

PURPLE LOOSESTRIFE
Lythrum salicaria

This European plant spreads very fast in wetlands here, creating spectacular scenes when in bloom. But it is also very destructive, crowding out native flowers valuable to birds and other wildlife.

LOOK FOR: A tall plant with crowded spikes of brilliant pinkish-lavender flowers; 4–6 crinkled petals and twice as many stamens.

LEAVES: Narrow, long (1¼–4"), in pairs or threes, seem to clasp stem.

HEIGHT: 2–5'.

BLOOMS: June–September.

HABITAT: Wetlands, roadsides.

RANGE: Northeast, Mid-Atlantic to Midwest, Northwest

FIREWEED
Epilobium angustifolium

LOOK FOR: Spires of deep pink flowers with 4 petals atop tall stems; top buds droop down. **HEIGHT:** 2–7'. **BLOOMS:** July–September. **HABITAT:** Burned areas. **RANGE:** Widespread except Southeast.

PRAIRIE BLAZING STAR
Liatris pycnostachya

LOOK FOR: Narrow, rose-purple cylinders of disk flowers crowded on a hairy, leafy stem. **HEIGHT:** 2–5'. **BLOOMS:** July–October. **HABITAT:** Prairies. **RANGE:** Central states.

DOTTED BLAZING STAR
Liatris punctata

LOOK FOR: Long, pointed, flat leaves (bracts) under flower heads. **HEIGHT:** 6–32". **BLOOMS:** August–September. **HABITAT:** Prairies. **RANGE:** Central North America.

125

ROCKY MOUNTAIN BEE PLANT
Cleome serrulata

L arge supplies of nectar inside this plant attract bees. It is also called Stinkweed because the leaves give off a skunky odor.

Look for: Cluster of pinkish to purplish and white flowers (each flower ½" long); 4 petals; 6 stamens; seedpod on a long protruding stalk from flower's center.

Leaves: Three lance-shaped leaflets, each ½–3" long.

Height: ½–5'.

Blooms: June–October.

Habitat: Plains, rangelands, and along roads.

Range: Northwest, Great Plains, Southwest.

ELEPHANT HEADS
Pedicularis groenlandica

Look for: Slender, tall spires of pink flowers shaped like little elephant heads. **Height:** Up to 28". **Blooms:** June–August. **Habitat:** Meadows and streams. **Range:** Western mountains, northern forest clearings.

YELLOW BEE PLANT
Cleome lutea

Look for: A cluster of small yellow flowers with 4 petals atop branched plant with leaflets arranged like fingers of a hand. **Height:** 1½–5'. **Blooms:** May–September. **Habitat:** Plains and valleys. **Range:** Western and southwestern regions.

127

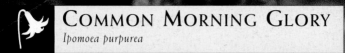

COMMON MORNING GLORY
Ipomoea purpurea

As its name implies, this flower opens at dawn and closes a few hours later. Its twining vine can wrap itself around crops, causing much damage.

Look for: A twining (twisting) vine of trumpet-shaped, purple, pink, blue, or white flowers, in clusters of 1–5; the 5 petals are joined together at the sides.

Leaves: 2–5" long; broad, heart-shaped; hairy stem.

Height: Climbs up to 10'.

Blooms: July–October.

Habitat: Fields, roadsides.

Range: Widespread.

Field Bindweed
Convolvulus arvensis

Look for: White, funnel-shaped flowers with purple lines on back; arrowhead-shaped leaves; twining stems. **Height:** 1–3'. **Blooms:** May–October. **Habitat:** Fields. **Range:** Widespread.

Beach Morning Glory
Calystegia soldanella

Look for: Pink, funnel-shaped flowers; fleshy stems; heart-shaped leaves; stays open all day. **Height:** Creeper, up to 20". **Blooms:** April–September. **Habitat:** Beaches. **Range:** West Coast.

Jimsonweed
Datura stramonium

Look for: White or violet, trumpet-shaped flowers; tall, rubbery stem; foul-smelling. **Height:** 1–5'. **Blooms:** July–October. **Habitat:** Fields. **Range:** Widespread. **Caution:** Poisonous.

RUGOSA ROSE
Rosa rugosa

Also called Wrinkled Rose, thanks to its wrinkly leaflets, this showy beauty first came from Asia. It is planted along beaches and dunes to help keep the sand from blowing away.

LOOK FOR: Large, rose-lavender or white flowers, with yellow stamens on prickly, hairy stems.

LEAVES: Long (3–6"), wrinkled, finely toothed leaflets.

HEIGHT: 4–6'.

BLOOMS: June–September.

HABITAT: Seashores, roadsides.

RANGE: Northeast to Midwest.

NOOTKA ROSE
Rosa nutkana

LOOK FOR: A shrub with light pink flowers; pairs of thorns. **HEIGHT:** 2–13'. **BLOOMS:** May–July. **HABITAT:** Woods, mountains. **RANGE:** Northwest.

PASTURE ROSE
Rosa carolina

LOOK FOR: Narrow, straight thorns on stems and large, pink flowers. **HEIGHT:** Less than 3". **BLOOMS:** June–July. **HABITAT:** Pastures, open woods. **RANGE:** East of the Rockies.

MULTIFLORA ROSE
Rosa multiflora

LOOK FOR: Clusters of small, white flowers; arching stems with curved thorns. **HEIGHT:** 3–6'. **BLOOMS:** May–June. **HABITAT:** Fields, roadsides. **RANGE:** East.

131

PRAIRIE GENTIAN
Eustoma grandiflorum

This flower's genus name comes from the Greek for "good" (*eu*) and "mouth" (*stoma*), calling attention to the wide opening that welcomes pollinators.

LOOK FOR: Large, bell-shaped, bluish-purplish flowers (1¼–1½" long) in clusters atop stems; 5 broad petals.

LEAVES: Oval, evenly spaced, in pairs with 3 obvious veins.

HEIGHT: 10–28".

BLOOMS: June–September.

HABITAT: Prairies, fields.

RANGE: Eastern Colorado to Nebraska; south to eastern New Mexico and Texas.

FRINGED GENTIAN
Gentiana detonsa

LOOK FOR: Blue-purple, tube-shaped flowers with 4 fringed petals opened wide; leaves in pairs. **HEIGHT:** 1–3'. **BLOOMS:** Late August–November. **HABITAT:** Meadows, bogs. **RANGE:** East and central states; western mountains. **ALERT:** Increasingly rare.

BOTTLE GENTIAN
Gentiana andrewsii

LOOK FOR: Clusters of dark blue to purple flowers with petals almost closed, nestled in the middle of 4 leaves atop stem. **HEIGHT:** 1–2'. **BLOOMS:** August–October. **HABITAT:** Wet meadows, fields, thickets. **RANGE:** East and central North America.

133

HAREBELL
Campanula rotundifolia

I f not pollinated by insects, the Harebell (also called Bluebell) can do the job by itself. Its pistil curls around to pick up loose pollen inside the flower cup.

Look for: Blue-to-purple bell-shaped flowers (¾" wide) nodding downward on thin stems; 5 petals, flaring outward; 5 purple stamens; in clusters or one to a stem.

Leaves: 3"-long, narrow stem leaves.

Height: 6–20".

Blooms: June–September.

Habitat: Rocky areas: slopes, meadows, shores.

Range: Northeastern and midwestern regions of North America; mountains of Southwest.

VIRGINIA BLUEBELL
Mertensia virginica

Look for: Bunches of pink buds that bloom to become light blue, horn-shaped flowers (¾–1" long); bunches hang from top of stem; wide, oval stem leaves. **Height:** 8–24". **Blooms:** March–June. **Habitat:** Wet woods. **Range:** East to central states.

MOUNTAIN BLUEBELL
Mertensia ciliata

Look for: Clusters of small, bellshaped, blue flowers turning pink with age (½–¾ long); clusters hang downward. **Height:** 6–60". **Blooms:** May–August. **Habitat:** Wet meadows, near streams. **Range:** Rocky Mountain and Sierra Nevada regions.

135

BLUE FLAG
Iris versicolor

YELLOW FLAG
Iris pseudacorus
LOOK FOR: A yellow flower, 3 veined sepals bending back, 3 vertical petals. **HEIGHT:** 2–3'. **BLOOMS:** June–August. **HABITAT:** Wetlands. **RANGE:** Widespread in East. **CAUTION:** Poisonous.

N amed for the Greek goddess of the rainbow, irises come in almost as many colors as the rainbow.

LOOK FOR: Violet-blue flowers with 3 bent-back, veined sepals with yellow patches and 3 narrower, vertical petals; each flower 2½–4" wide; 3 stamens.

LEAVES: Long (8–32") and narrow, growing upward from base (sword-like).

HEIGHT: 2–3'.

BLOOMS: May–July.

HABITAT: Marshes, wet meadows.

RANGE: Southern Canada; Great Lakes areas; northeast to Mid-Atlantic states.

CAUTION: Underground stem (rhizome) is poisonous.

ROCKY MOUNTAIN IRIS
Iris missouriensis
LOOK FOR: Large blue-violet flowers with 3 petals in center; 3 sepals curve down. **HEIGHT:** 8–20". **BLOOMS:** May–June. **HABITAT:** Meadows. **RANGE:** West. **CAUTION:** Poisonous.

RED IRIS
Iris fulva
LOOK FOR: Reddish-brown flowers with veins. **HEIGHT:** 2–5'. **BLOOMS:** May–June. **HABITAT:** Wetlands. **RANGE:** Illinois to Alabama and Louisiana. **CAUTION:** Poisonous.

PICKERELWEED
Pontederia cordata

Found in quiet, shallow freshwater, this flower's common name suggests the kind of fish it shares its home with—pickerel.

Look for: Violet-blue flower spikes and glossy leaves growing above the water; each funnel-shaped flower is ⅓" long; 1 upper petal has 2 yellow spots.

Leaves: 4–10" long; heart-shaped; grow above water; 1 leaf on flower stalk.

Height: Stalk 1–2' above water.

Blooms: June–November.

Habitat: Marshes, ponds, lakes, and streams.

Range: Widespread from Minnesota to East Coast.

WATER HYACINTH
Eichhornia crassipes

Look for: A blue-violet spike growing above the water; flowers larger than pickerelweed's (2" wide) with yellow spot on upper petal; leafstalks float. **Height:** Up to 16" above water. **Blooms:** All year. **Habitat:** Marshes, streams, swamps, lakes. **Range:** Virginia to Florida; west to Texas and Missouri.

COMMON CAMAS
Camassia quamash

Look for: A vertical cluster of blue-to-purple flowers at top of leafless stem; each star-shaped flower, 1½–2½" wide, on its own short stem attached to central stem; long, narrow leaves clustered around base of central stem. **Height:** 12–20". **Blooms:** April–June. **Habitat:** Wet meadows. **Range:** Western regions.

WILD LUPINE
Lupinus perennis

Named after *lupus*, the Latin word for wolf, lupines were unjustly accused of "wolfing" nutrients from the soil. Just the opposite is true. Lupines improve the soil by increasing its nitrogen content.

Look for: Blue-purple spire of flowers, each up to ⅔" long; one upper petal has a pale spot in the center.

Leaves: 7–11 leaflets (each to 2" long) around a central spot, like spokes in a wheel.

Height: 8–24".

Blooms: April–July.

Habitat: Open woods, fields.

Range: Widespread from Minnesota to East Coast.

Alert: Wild Lupine is becoming rare.

PURPLE LOCO
Oxytropis lambertii

Look for: Sweet-scented, pink-to-lavender flowers on leafless stalk in center of ring of hairy leaves.
Height: 8–12".
Blooms: May–July.
Habitat: Prairies.
Range: Southwest Canada; central states. **Caution:** Poisonous.

TEXAS BLUEBONNET
Lupinus subcarnosus

Look for: A spike of blue flowers; a pale, yellowish area on upper petal that reddens with age.
Height: 12–15".
Blooms: April–May.
Habitat: Grasslands.
Range: Texas.

HAIRY VETCH
Vicia villosa

Look for: A climbing vine with hairy stem; cluster of violet-white flowers on 1 side of stem. **Height:** Vine to 3'. **Blooms:** May–October. **Habitat:** Fields. **Range:** East of the Rockies.

TRUE FORGET-ME-NOT
Myosotis scorpioides

L egend has it that a suitor was tragically lost in a raging current as he tried to pick this flower for his love. His last words to her were "Forget me not!" Forget him, she never did.

Look for: Small sky-blue flowers with yellow center. Hairy stem divides into 2 branches near the top, separating as the flowers bloom.

Leaves: 1–2" long; oblong, hairy.

Height: 6–24".

Blooms: May–October.

Habitat: Wet places.

Range: Widespread.

Sky Pilot
Polemonium viscosum

Look for: Bell-shaped flowers with small leaflets that form fuzzy tubes; skunky scent.
Height: 4–16".
Blooms: June–August.
Habitat: Mountains.
Range: Northwest, Rocky Mountains.

Blue-eyed Grass
Sisyrinchium angustifolium

Look for: Six blue, pointed petals; grass-like leaves.
Height: 4–20".
Blooms: May–July.
Habitat: Meadows, marshes, shores.
Range: Widespread.

Many-flowered Stickseed
Hackelia floribunda

Look for: Small, light blue flowers with central yellow pads; prickles on nuts. **Height:** 1–3'.
Blooms: June–August. **Habitat:** Forests. **Range:** West, Southwest.

143

WILD BLUE PHLOX
Phlox divaricata

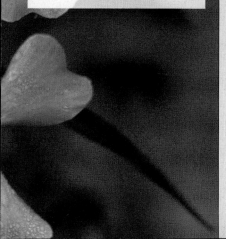

The Wild Blue Phlox growing in the eastern half of its range has a triangular cut in each petal; the ones found more westward do not. Also called Wild Sweet William.

Look for: Cluster of pale blue to lavender flowers (¾–1½" wide) atop a sticky stem; 5 flat petals arranged in a pinwheel shape; 5 stamens.

Leaves: 1–2" long; in pairs; oval to lance-shaped.

Height: 10–20".

Blooms: April–June.

Habitat: Woods, fields.

Range: East, Mid-Atlantic.

PERIWINKLE (MYRTLE)
Vinca minor

Look for: Low, trailing plant with white star in center of 5 purplish-blue petals; shiny, dark leaves. **Height:** 6–8". **Blooms:** April–May. **Habitat:** Woods, roadsides. **Range:** East of the Rockies.

LONG-LEAVED PHLOX
Phlox longifolia

Look for: Pink, pale lilac, or white flowers; 5 flat petals form pinwheel shape; shorter than Wild Blue Phlox. **Height:** 4–16". **Blooms:** April–July. **Habitat:** Rocky places. **Range:** West.

145

How to use the reference section

Swamp Rose

The **Glossary** beginning on the opposite page contains terms used by botanists and naturalists. If you run across a word in this book that you don't understand, check the glossary for a definition. Also in this section is a listing of **Resources**, including books, Web sites, and organizations devoted to North American wildflowers. Finally, there is an **Index** of all the species covered in the Field Guide section of this book.

The 50 state flowers

Every state has its official flower. All 50 state flowers appear on the next five pages listed in alphabetical order by state. If you live in Missouri, for example, go across the list to the states beginning with the letter M; the state flower for Missouri is the Red Hawthorn. Like the Red Hawthorn, many other state flowers are flowering trees and not wildflowers. (Wildflowers are defined in this book as flowering plants—including shrubs, vines, and cacti—but not trees and garden flowers.) The names in this list are those used by the states and may not be the common names used by botanists.

Achene
A small, dry, hard fruit that does not open and contains one seed.

Anther
The tip of a flower's stamen that produces pollen grains.

Barb
A short, hooked bristle.

Basal
At the base of (a stem, leaf, or plant).

Bog
An area of wet, spongy ground, usually with peat moss and evergreen trees, such as black spruce and various cedars.

Bracts
Modified leaves, usually smaller than the leaves on the stem, located at the base of a flower.

Calyx
All the sepals together, usually green in color.

Carnivorous
Meat-eating. Some plants trap, dissolve, and digest insects.

Chlorophyll
Green-colored matter (pigment) in most plants' leaves that absorbs the energy from sunlight; it is necessary for the process of photosynthesis.

Composite flower
A flower such as a daisy or a dandelion composed of many flowers arranged in a dense head.

Cross-pollination
The transfer of pollen from one plant to the stigma of another.

Cultivated
Plants that people have developed or tended, such as flowering plants in a garden.

Disk flowers
Small, tubular flowers at the center of a composite flower, such as the center of a Common Sunflower.

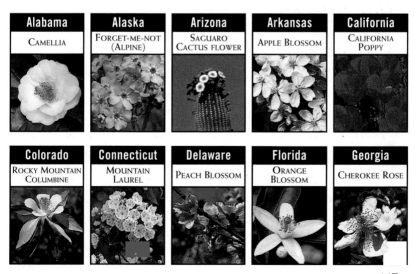

Alabama	Alaska	Arizona	Arkansas	California
CAMELLIA	FORGET-ME-NOT (ALPINE)	SAGUARO CACTUS FLOWER	APPLE BLOSSOM	CALIFORNIA POPPY

Colorado	Connecticut	Delaware	Florida	Georgia
ROCKY MOUNTAIN COLUMBINE	MOUNTAIN LAUREL	PEACH BLOSSOM	ORANGE BLOSSOM	CHEROKEE ROSE

GLOSSARY AND THE 50 STATE FLOWERS

Dormant period
A rest period when all growth stops. Many plants are dormant in the winter months.

Duff
Partly-decayed organic (plant or animal) matter on the forest floor.

Fertilization
The process of reproduction by which male cells combine with female cells in a flower's ovary after pollination.

Filament
The stalk part of a stamen that holds up the anther.

Floss
A silky, thread-like substance on some plants, such as milkweed.

Flower head
Many flowers in a bunch at the top of a stem.

Fruit
The ripened ovary and the seeds within it.

Genus
A group of closely related species. *Genera* is the plural form of *genus*.

Germinate
To sprout from seed or spore.

Grasslands
An area of prairie or meadow grass, usually on flat or gently rolling plains that are relatively dry most of the year.

Habitat
A place where a plant or animal is normally found.

Immigrants
Plants that have been introduced to a region. For example, many plants were brought to North America from Europe by colonists.

Leaflet
A small, leaf-like part of a compound leaf.

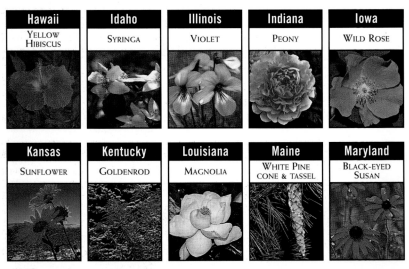

Hawaii	Idaho	Illinois	Indiana	Iowa
YELLOW HIBISCUS	SYRINGA	VIOLET	PEONY	WILD ROSE

Kansas	Kentucky	Louisiana	Maine	Maryland
SUNFLOWER	GOLDENROD	MAGNOLIA	WHITE PINE CONE & TASSEL	BLACK-EYED SUSAN

Marsh

A wetland with tall grasses. A marsh is dominated by grass; a swamp by trees such as Bald Cypresses.

Natives

Plants that originated in a particular region. Cacti, for example, are native to North America.

Nectar

The sweet liquid produced by flowers that attracts insects and other pollinators.

Nocturnal

Active at night, such as a plant whose flowers open during the night.

Ovary

A tiny chamber at the bottom of the pistil where seeds develop.

Ovules

The eggs of a plant, which, when fertilized, become seeds.

Palmate

With leaflets arranged like the fingers on a hand.

Petals

Leaf-like structures surrounding the male and female parts of a flower. The whorl of petals may form different shapes, including a cup, a bell, or a tube.

Photosynthesis

The process by which plants use sunlight to convert water and carbon dioxide into a sugary food called *glucose* that plants need. Oxygen (that we breathe) and water vapor are given off by plants during this process.

Pinnate

With leaflets on each side of a common stem.

Pistil

The female part of a flower, made up of the stigma, style, and ovary.

Pod

A seed covering that dries

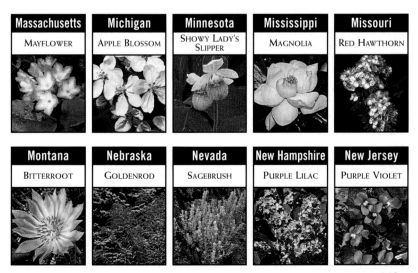

Massachusetts	Michigan	Minnesota	Mississippi	Missouri
MAYFLOWER	APPLE BLOSSOM	SHOWY LADY'S SLIPPER	MAGNOLIA	RED HAWTHORN

Montana	Nebraska	Nevada	New Hampshire	New Jersey
BITTERROOT	GOLDENROD	SAGEBRUSH	PURPLE LILAC	PURPLE VIOLET

out and opens when the seed matures.

Pollen
The part of the male flower that is carried to other flowers for fertilization.

Pollination
The transfer of pollen from an anther to a stigma.

Ray flowers
Individual flowers that resemble single petals, surrounding a central group of disk flowers. Each "petal" of a daisy is a ray flower.

Rhizome
An underground stem that often grows horizontally and sends up shoots.

Rosette
A cluster of leaves arranged in a circle at the base of the plant.

Saprophyte
A plant that lacks chlorophyll (green coloration) and lives on dead organic matter, usually found in deep, shady woods.

Self-pollination
A process by which the pollen of a flower lands on the stigma of the same plant.

Sepals
Leaf-like structures underneath the flower. Sepals are usually green but can resemble petals.

Spadix
A club-like spike that bears flowers, such as the central spadix of a Jack-in-the-Pulpit.

Spathe
A leaf-like bract that encloses a flower like a hood.

Species
A group of plants or animals that interbreeds and produces offspring. Similar species are grouped as a genus.

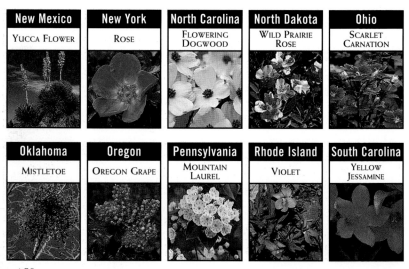

New Mexico	New York	North Carolina	North Dakota	Ohio
YUCCA FLOWER	ROSE	FLOWERING DOGWOOD	WILD PRAIRIE ROSE	SCARLET CARNATION

Oklahoma	Oregon	Pennsylvania	Rhode Island	South Carolina
MISTLETOE	OREGON GRAPE	MOUNTAIN LAUREL	VIOLET	YELLOW JESSAMINE

Spur
A small, slender sac formed by an extension of petals or sepals, often holding nectar, such as in the orchid.

Stamen
The male part of the flower, made up of a filament and an anther.

Stigma
The tip of the pistil that receives pollen.

Stomata
Tiny holes on the underside of a leaf through which carbon dioxide from the air is absorbed and oxygen escapes.

Style
The stalk-like (tube) part of the pistil that receives the pollen and connects the ovary and stigma.

Succulent
Having thick, fleshy leaves that store water.

Toothed
Having a jagged edge (as in a "toothed" leaf).

Trifoliate
With leaflets arranged in groups of three on a common stem.

Ultraviolet
Wavelengths just beyond the vision of people. Some insects can see ultraviolet light.

Vegetative propagation
Reproduction by roots, runners, bulbs, and shoots, rather than by seeds.

Wetlands
Damp or wet ground, such as a bog or swamp.

Whorl
Three or more leaves growing at the same point on a stem.

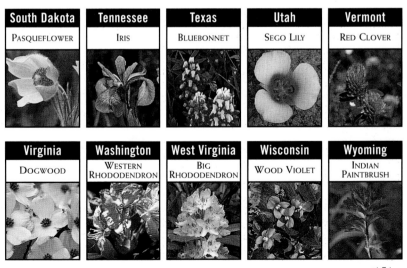

South Dakota	Tennessee	Texas	Utah	Vermont
PASQUEFLOWER	IRIS	BLUEBONNET	SEGO LILY	RED CLOVER

Virginia	Washington	West Virginia	Wisconsin	Wyoming
DOGWOOD	WESTERN RHODODENDRON	BIG RHODODENDRON	WOOD VIOLET	INDIAN PAINTBRUSH

RESOURCES

FOR FURTHER READING

Dandelion, Pokeweed, and Goosefoot: How the Early Settlers Used Plants for Food, Medicine, and in the Home
Elizabeth Scheaffer
Young Scott Books, 1972

Eyewitness Books: Plants
David Burnie
Alfred A. Knopf, 1989

Flowers
(Eyewitness Explorers Series)
David Burnie
Dorling Kindersley, 1992

Flowers
(First Discovery Books)
Rene Mettler and Gallimard Jeunesse
Scholastic Inc., 1993

Flowers
(Golden Guide Series)
Alexander C. Martin and Herbert S. Zim
Golden Books, 1987

Flowers
(Naturebook Series)
Ivan Anatta
Childs World, Inc., 1993

Flowers
(Walkabout Series)
Henry Pluckrose
Children's Press, 1994

From Flower to Fruit
Anne Ophelia Dowden
Crowell Junior Books, 1984

A Guide to Enjoying Wildflowers
(Stokes Nature Guides)
Donald Stokes and Lillian Stokes
Little, Brown & Co., 1985

Hedgemaids and Fairy Candles: The Lives and Lore of North American Wildflowers
Jack Sanders
Ragged Mountain Press, 1993

The History and Folklore of North American Wildflowers
Timothy Coffey
Houghton Mifflin Co., 1993

National Audubon Society Beginner Guide: Wildflowers of North America
Random House, 1982

National Audubon Society Field Guide to North American Wildflowers (Eastern Region)
William A. Niering and Nancy C. Olmstead
Alfred A. Knopf, 1994

National Audubon Society Field Guide to North American Wildflowers (Western Region)
Richard Spellenberg
Alfred A. Knopf, 1994

National Audubon Society Pocket Guide to Familiar Flowers of North America (Eastern Region)
Richard Spellenberg
Alfred A. Knopf, 1986

National Audubon Society Pocket Guide to Familiar Flowers of North America (Western Region)

Common Sunflower page 76

Richard Spellenberg
Alfred A. Knopf, 1996

Nature in a Nutshell for Kids
Jean Potter
John Wiley & Sons, 1995

Nature Smart: A Family Guide to Nature
Stan Tekiela and Karen Shanberg
Adventure Publications, 1994

Naturewatch: Exploring Nature with Your Children
Adrienne Katz
Addison-Wesley, 1986

Newcomb's Wildflower Guide
Lawrence Newcomb and Gordon Morrison (Illustrator)
Little, Brown & Co., 1989

North American Wildlife
(An Illustrated Guide to 2,000 Plants and Animals)
Reader's Digest, 1996

True Forget-me-not page 142

Plant Families
Carol Lerner
William Morrow & Co., Inc.,
1989

Plant Science
Boy Scouts of America, 1985

Poisons in Our Path: Plants that Harm and Heal
Anne Ophelia Dowden
HarperCollins, 1994

Seeds: Pop, Stick, Glide
Patricia Lauber
Crown, 1981

State Flowers
Anne Ophelia Dowden
Crowell Junior Books, 1978

Usborne Mysteries and Marvels of Plant Life
Barbara Cook
EDC Publishing, 1989

Wildflora of the Northeast
Anita and Spider Barbour
Overlook Press, 1995

Wildflower ABC
Diana Pomeroy
Harcourt Brace, 1997

Wildflower Field Guide & Press for Kids
Carol A. Cambell
Workman Publishing Co., 1993

Wildflowers
(Peterson First Guides)
Roger Tory Peterson
Houghton Mifflin Co., 1987

Wildflowers
(Science Nature Guide Series)
Pam Forey
Thunder Bay Press, 1994

Wildflowers
(Spotter's Guide Series)

C. Humphries
EDC Publishing, 1993

Wildflowers: A Garden Primer
Anne Velghe
Farrar, Straus & Giroux, Inc.,
1994

Wildflowers and the Stories Behind Their Names
Phyllis S. Busch
Charles Scribner's Sons, 1977

Wildflowers of the Southern Appalachians
Kevin Adams and Marty Castevens
John R. Blair, 1996

ORGANIZATIONS

Missouri Botanical Gardens
PO Box 229
St. Louis, MO
63166-0299
Tel: (314) 577-5100
http://www.mobot.org

National Audubon Society
700 Broadway
New York, NY 10003-9562
Tel: 212-979-3000
1-800-274-4201
E-mail: tcanela@audubon.org

National Wildflower Research Center
4801 La Crosse Avenue
Austin, TX 78739
Tel: 512-292-4100
nwrc@onr.com

New England Wildflower Society
180 Hemenway Road
Framingham, MA
Tel: 508 877-7630
http://www.newfs.org/~newfs
E-mail: newfs@newfs.org

New York Botanical Gardens
200 Street and Southern Blvd.

Bronx, NY
Tel: 718-817-8700
www.nybg.org

WEB SITES

Joe & Mindy's Wildflower Links
www.nhn.uoknor.edu/~howard/
wildflwr2.html

Michigan Electronic Library-Wildflowers
mel.lib.mi.us/science/wild.html

Missouri Botanical Garden
www.mobot.org

National Wildflower Research Center
www.wildflower.org

New York Botanical Gardens
www.nybg.org

North American Wildflowers (Channel Marketmakers photosite)
www.cmm1.com/photos/titles/12
700.html

Spring Larkspur

INDEX

Red Clover page 120

INDEX

Female Ruby-throated
Hummingbird and
Bee Balm

Blue Columbine

PHOTO/ILLUSTRATION CREDITS

Photo credits are listed by page from left to right, top to bottom.

Half-title page: Gerald & Buff Corsi/Focus on Nature, Inc.
Title page: Mark Turner
Table of contents: Frank Oberle
6: Paul Rezendes
8a: Special Collections, California Academy of Sciences
8b: L. West/Photo Researchers*
9: David Bashaw
10a: Frank Oberle
10b: Simpson & Co. Nature Stock
10c: Dr. E. R. Degginger/Photo Researchers
10d: Fletcher & Baylis/Photo Researchers
11a: Stan Goldblatt/Photo Researchers
11b: E. R. Degginger/Color-Pic, Inc.
11c: E. R. Degginger/Color-Pic, Inc.
11d: Michael M. Smith/View Two Plus
11e: Jim Roetzel
12a: Stephen G. Maka
12b (Wild Rose): L. West/Photo Researchers
12c: Frank Oberle
13a: David Bashaw
13b: Geoff Bryant/Photo Researchers
14–15: Rod Planck/Photo Researchers
15a: Gregory G. Dimijian/Photo Researchers
15b: David Bashaw
15c: Joy Spurr
16a: Michael M. Smith/View Two Plus
16b: Tom C. Boyden
16c: Greg Gorel
17a: Michael P. Gadomski/Photo Researchers
17b: Joy Spurr
18 a,d: David Bashaw
18b: Simpson & Co. Nature Stock
18c: James H. Robinson
19a: Allen Blake Sheldon
19b: David Bashaw
19c (Buttercup): John Buitenkant/Photo Researchers
19d: Simpson & Co. Nature Stock
20a: Scott Camazine/Photo Researchers
20b: Tom McHugh/Photo Researchers
20c: Mark Turner
21a: David Ransow
21b: Paul Rezendes
21c: Stephen P. Parker/Photo Researchers
22a: Carl von Linne/Mary Evans Picture Library/Photo Researchers
22b: David Liebman
23a: E. R. Degginger/Color-Pic, Inc.
23b: Adam Jones/Photo Researchers
23c: Ken Brate/Photo Researchers
23d: E. R. Degginger/Color-Pic, Inc.
24a: Gilbert Grant/Photo Researchers
24b: C.K. Lorenz/Photo Researchers
24c: Anthony Mercieca/Photo Researchers
24–25 (Forget-me-not): Gail Jankus/Photo Researchers
25a: Ron Austing
25b: Richard Parker/Photo Researchers
25c: M.W.F. Tweedie/Photo Researchers
25d: M.W.F. Tweedie/Photo Researchers
25e: Michael P. Gadomski/Photo Researchers
26a: Rod Planck/Photo Researchers
26b (Buttercup): Tom Branch/Photo

Researchers
26c: Ron Austing
27a: Simpson & Co. Nature Stock
27b: Dennis Flaherty
27c (Elephant Heads): Robert E. Barber
27d (Iris): Rod Planck/Photo Researchers
27e (Golden Alexander): Paul Rezendes
28–29: David Bashaw
30a: John Serrao
30b: Paul Rezendes
30c: Joseph G. Strauch, Jr.
30d: Treat Davidson/Photo Researchers
31a: Nuridsany & Perennou/Photo Researchers
31b: Herbert Clarke
31c: Stephen P. Parker/Photo Researchers
31d: E. R. Degginger/Color-Pic, Inc.
32a: Dennis Flaherty
32b (Bee Balm): Nick Bergkessel/Photo Researchers
32c (Trillium): Kevin Adams
33a: Joseph G. Strauch, Jr.
33b: Harry M. Walker
33c: Darrell Gulin
33d: Wolfgang Kaehler
34a: Emily Johnson
34b: Joseph G. Strauch, Jr.
34c: James H. Robinson
35a (Woods): Rod Planck/Photo Researchers
35b: Kent & Donna Dannen/Photo Researchers
36a: James R. Fisher/Photo Researchers
36b: Tom & Pat Leeson/Photo Researchers
36c (Grassland): Tom & Pat Leeson/Photo Researchers
37a: E. R. Degginger/Color-Pic, Inc.
37b: Edna Douthat/Photo Researchers
37c: Ronald J. Taylor
38a: E. R. Degginger/Color-Pic, Inc.
38b: Mark Turner
38c: James H. Robinson/Photo Researchers
38–39: Jeff Lepore/Photo Researchers
39a: Stephen G. Maka
39b: Ray Packard
39c: Kevin Adams
40a: Rob Curtis/The Early Birder
40b: Karl H. Switak/Photo Researchers
40c: Gregory Ochocki/Photo Researchers
41a: Leonard Lee Rue III/Photo Researchers
41b: Londie G. Padelsky
41c: Jim Steinberg/Photo Researchers
42a: Darryl R. Beers
42b: Holt Studios Ltd/Photo Researchers
43a: Jeff Lepore/Photo Researchers
43b: Leonard Lee Rue III/Photo Researchers
43c: Michael M. Smith/View Two Plus
43d: Stephen J. Krasemann/Photo Researchers
44a: Adam Jones/Photo Researchers
44b: Tom C. Boyden
46: Simpson & Co. Nature Stock
47a: Michael M. Smith/View Two Plus
47b: Paul Rezendes
48: Charles Webb
49a: Gerald and Buff Corsi/Focus on Nature, Inc.
49b: Simpson & Co. Nature Stock
49c: Simpson & Nature Stock
50: Daniel W. Mathews
51a: Darrell Gulin

51b: Kevin Adams
52: Michael P. Gadomski/Photo Researchers
53a: Joy Spurr
53b: Emily Johnson
53c: Tom Branch/Photo Researchers
54: Rod Planck/Photo Researchers
55a: Francis E. Caldwell
55b: Michael M. Smith/View Two Plus
56: Andrew J. Martinez
57a: Robert E. Barber
57b: Eliot Cohen
58: Patrick W. Grace/Photo Researchers
59a: Walt Anderson
59b: C. K. Lorenz/Photo Researchers
60: Mark Turner
61a: Dennis Flaherty
61b: Dr. P. J. McLaughlin/Photo Researchers
61c: John Bova/Photo Researchers
62: Michael P. Gadomski/Photo Researchers
63a: Kent & Donna Dannen/Photo Researchers
63b: John A. Lynch
63c: Jeff Lepore/Photo Researchers
64: Scott Camazine/Photo Researchers
65a: John Serrao
65b: Joy Spurr
66: Jerry Pavia
67a: Frank Oberle
67b: Kevin Adams
67c: Joy Spurr
68: Michael P. Gadomski/Photo Researchers
69a: Gary W. Carter
69b: Gerald & Buff Corsi/Focus on Nature, Inc.
70: Rob Curtis/The Early Birder
71a: Harry M. Walker
71b: E. R. Degginger/Color-Pic, Inc.
71c: Karl H. Switak/Photo Researchers
72: George E. Jones III/Photo Researchers
73a: Frank Oberle
73b: Joy Spurr
73c: Simpson & Co. Nature Stock
74: Jim Zipp/Photo Researchers
75a: Mark Turner
75b: Joseph G. Strauch, Jr.
75c: Wolfgang Kaehler
76: John Eastcott/Yva Momatiuk/Photo Researchers
77a: S. R. Maglione/Photo Researchers
77b: Michael P. Gadomski/Photo Researchers
77c: Scott T. Smith
78: Alan and Linda Detrick
79a: Michael Lustbader/Photo Researchers
79b: Ronald J. Taylor
80: Simpson & Co. Nature Stock
81a: John Serrao
81b: Gerald & Buff Corsi/Focus on Nature, Inc.
81c: Darryl R. Beers
82: Joy Spurr
83a: Joseph G. Strauch, Jr.
83b: Noble Proctor/Photo Researchers
84: Richard Parker/Photo Researchers
85a: Michael P. Gadomski/Photo Researchers
85b: Kent & Donna Dannen/Photo Researchers
85c: Emily Johnson
86: Sally Weigand
87a: Gerald & Buff Corsi/Focus on Nature,

Prepared and produced by
Chanticleer Press, Inc., and Chic Simple Design

Founder, Chanticleer Press, Inc.: Paul Steiner

Publisher, Chanticleer Press, Inc.: Andrew Stewart
Publishers, Chic Simple Design: Jeff Stone, Kim Johnson Gross

Chanticleer Staff:
Editor-in-Chief: Amy K. Hughes
Director of Production: Alicia Mills
Production Associate: Philip Pfeifer
Photo Editor: Zan Carter
Senior Editor: Lauren Weidenman
Managing Editors: Kristina Lucenko and Edie Locke
Editorial Assistant: Karin Murphy

Project Editors: Edward S. Barnard, Sharon Fass Yates
Bookmark Associates, Inc.

Chic Simple Design Staff:
Art Direction/Design: Takuyo Takahashi
Production/Design: Jinger Peissig
Project Coordinator: Gillian Oppenheim
Production: Camilla Marstrand
Design Interns: Kathryn Hammill, Danielle Huthart,
Diane Shaw, Sylvie Pusztaszeri

Writer (The world of wildflowers, How to look at wildflowers, Field guide): Susan Hood
Consultant: Brian Cassie, Massachusetts Audubon Society
Copy Editors: Kristina Bohl, Sarah Burns
Illustrator: Taina Litwak
Icon Illustrator: Holly Kowitt
Studio Photographer: David Bashaw

Scholastic Inc. Staff:
Editorial Director: Wendy Barish, Creative Director: David Saylor,
Managing Editor: Manuela Soares, Production Editor: Sean Gallagher,
Manufacturing Manager: Janet Castiglione

Original Series Design: Chic Simple Design, Takuyo Takahashi